INSTANT Piano Songs

Audio Access
Included

CHRISTMAS STANDARDS

Simple Sheet Music + Audio Play-Along

T0084212

PLAYBACK+
Speed • Pitch • Balance • Loop

To access audio visit:
www.halleonard.com/mylibrary
Enter Code
"3592-6163-1002-2169"

ISBN 978-1-5400-5427-2

Visit Hal Leonard Online at
www.halleonard.com

Contact us:
Hal Leonard
7777 West Bluemound Road
Milwaukee, WI 53213
Email: info@halleonard.com

In Europe, contact:
Hal Leonard Europe Limited
42 Wigmore Street
Marylebone, London, W1U 2RN
Email: info@halleonardeurope.com

In Australia, contact:
Hal Leonard Australia Pty. Ltd.
4 Lentara Court
Cheltenham, Victoria, 3192 Australia
Email: info@halleonard.com.au

CONTENTS

Welcome to the *INSTANT Piano Songs* series!

This unique, flexible collection allows you to play with either one hand or two. Three playing options are available—all of which sound great with the online backing tracks:

1. **Play only the melody with your right hand.**

2. **Add basic chords in your left hand, which are notated for you.**

3. **Use suggested rhythm patterns for the left-hand chords.**

Letter names appear inside the notes in both hands to assist you, and there are no key signatures to worry about. If a **sharp** ♯ or **flat** ♭ is needed, it is shown beside the note each time, even within the same measure.

If two notes are connected by a **tie** ⌣, hold the first note for the combined number of beats. (The second note does not show a letter name since it is not re-struck.)

Sometimes the melody needs to be played an octave higher to avoid overlapping with the left-hand chords. (If your starting note is C, the next C to the right is one octave higher.) If you are using only your right hand, however, you can disregard this instruction in the music.

🔊 The backing tracks are designed to enhance the piano arrangements, regardless of how you choose to play them. Each track includes two measures of count-off clicks at the beginning. If the recording is too fast or too slow, use the online *PLAYBACK+* player to adjust it to a more comfortable tempo (speed).

Optional left-hand rhythm patterns are provided for when you are ready to move beyond the basic chords. The patterns are based on the three notes of the basic chords and appear as small, gray notes in the first line of each song. Feel free to use the suggested pattern throughout the song, or create your own. Sample rhythm patterns are shown below. (Of course, you can always play just the basic chords if you wish!)

Have fun! Whether you play with one hand or two, you'll sound great!

Sample Rhythm Patterns

4/4 Meter

3/4 Meter

6/8 Meter

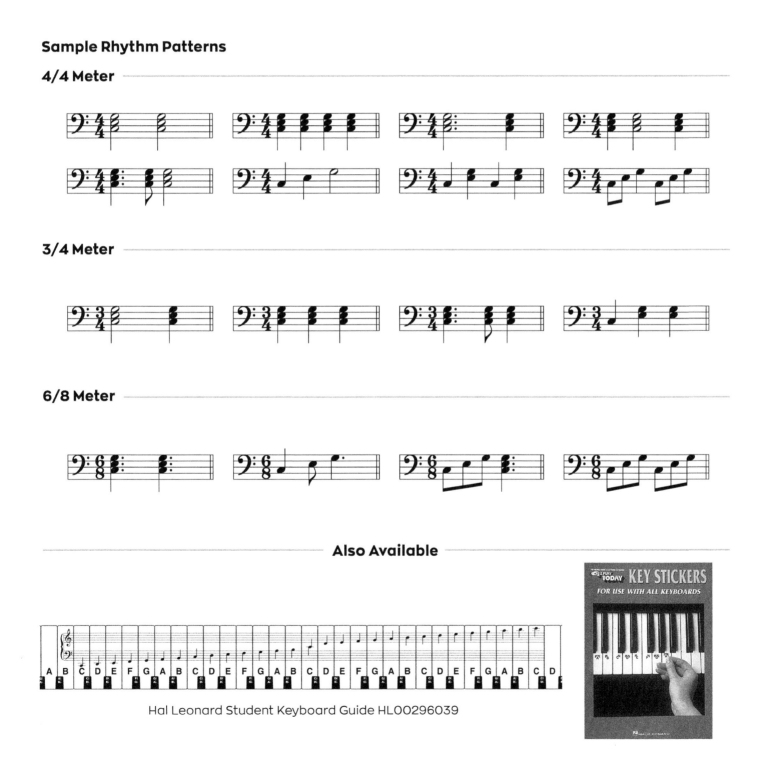

Also Available

Hal Leonard Student Keyboard Guide HL00296039

Key Stickers HL00100016

All I Want for Christmas Is My Two Front Teeth

Words and Music by
Don Gardner

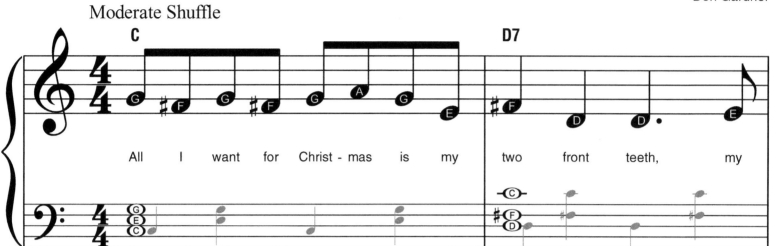

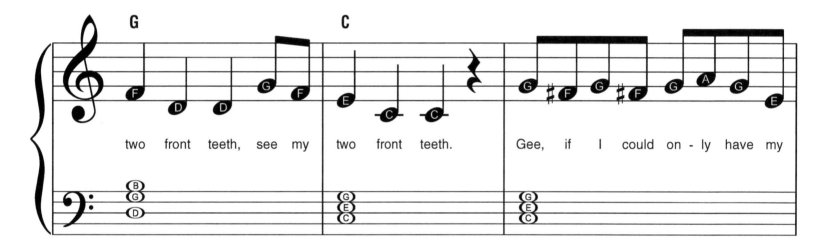

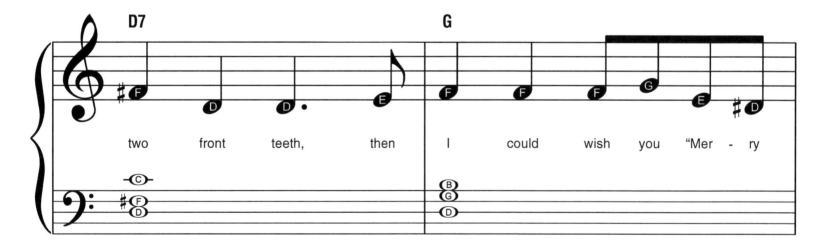

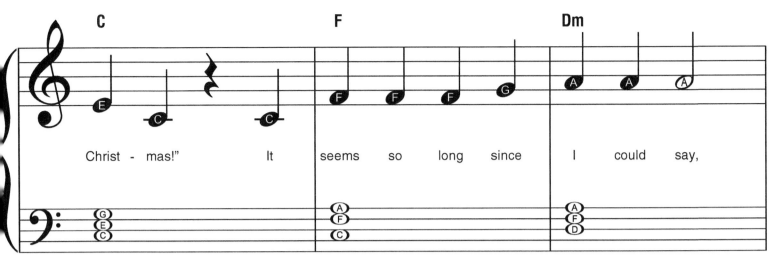

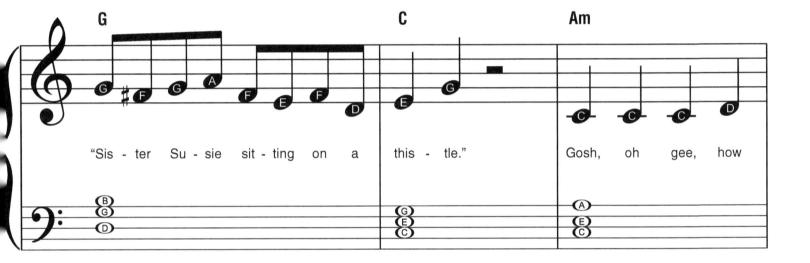

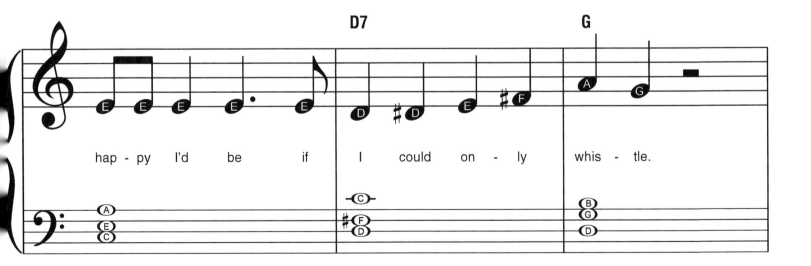

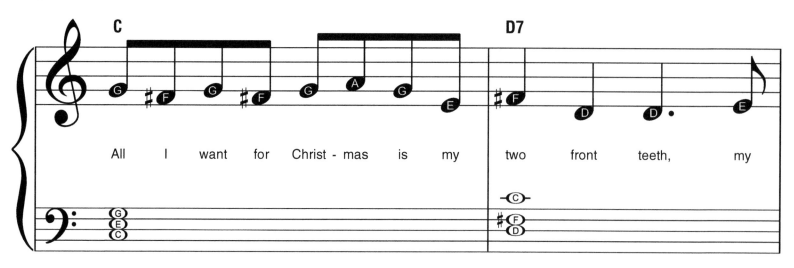

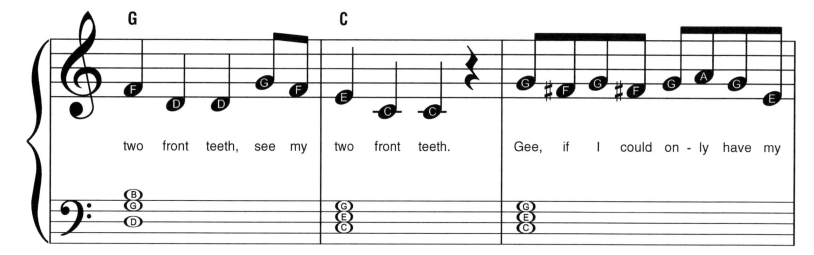

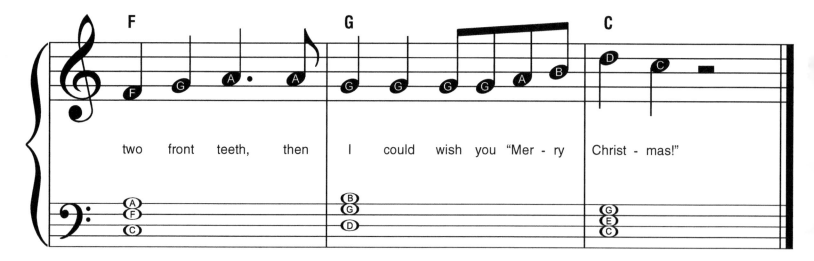

All I Want for Christmas Is You

Words and Music by Mariah Carey
and Walter Afanasieff

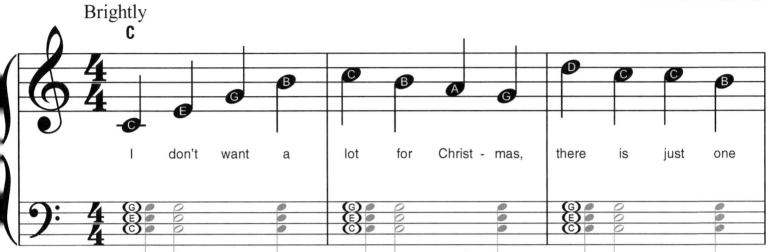

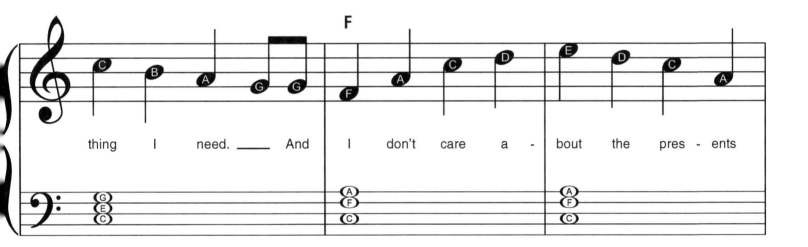

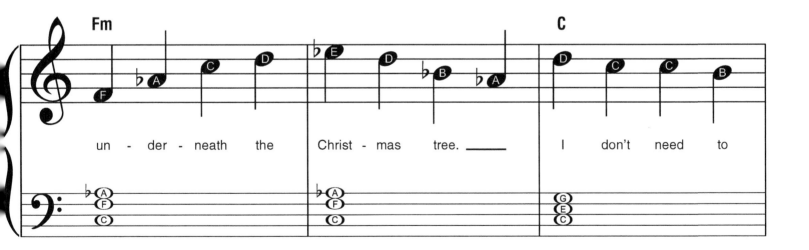

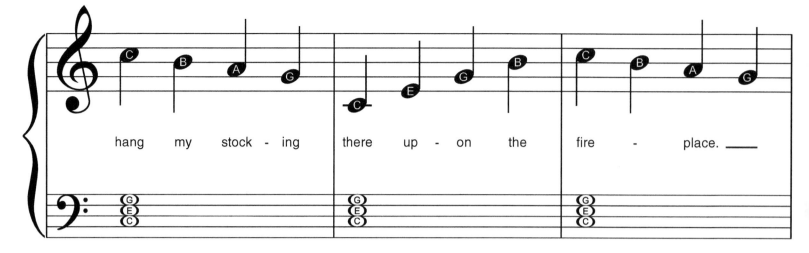

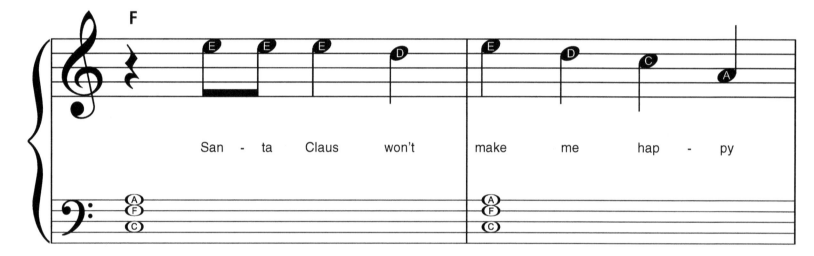

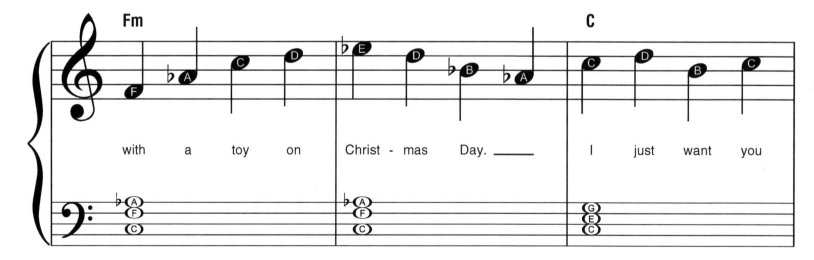

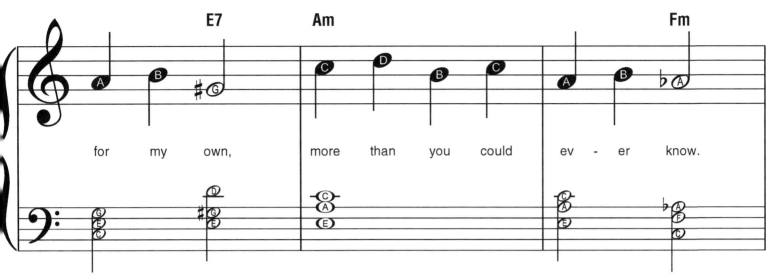

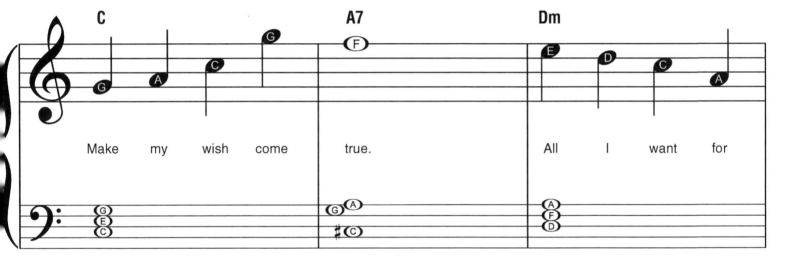

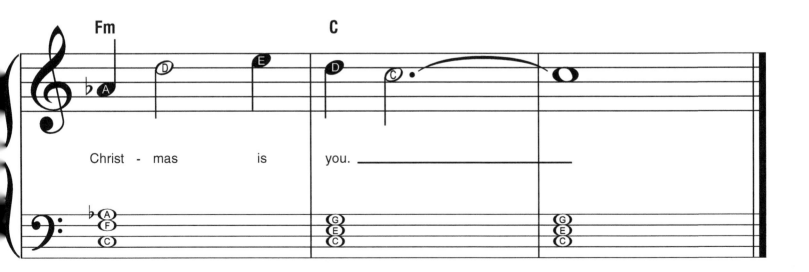

Blue Christmas

Words and Music by Billy Hayes
and Jay Johnson

Sad Shuffle
(no chord)

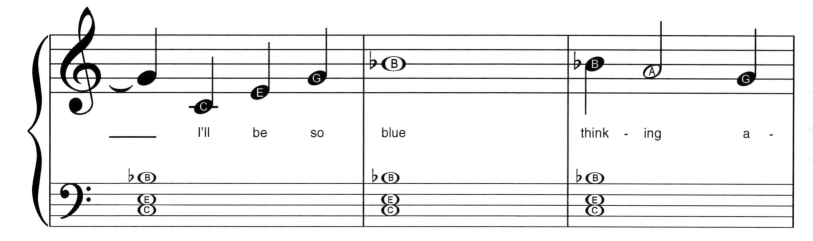

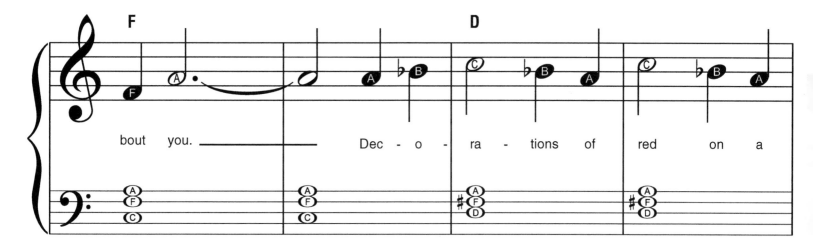

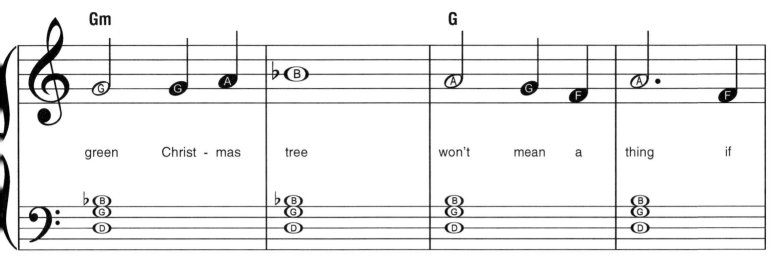

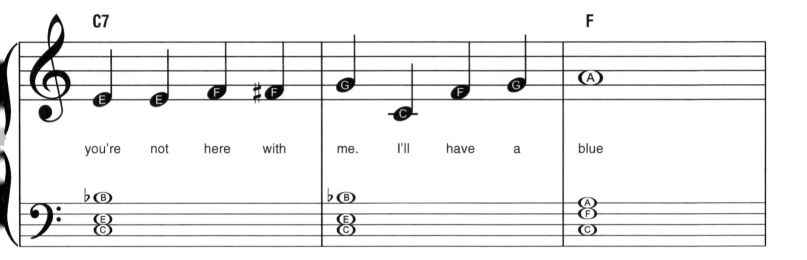

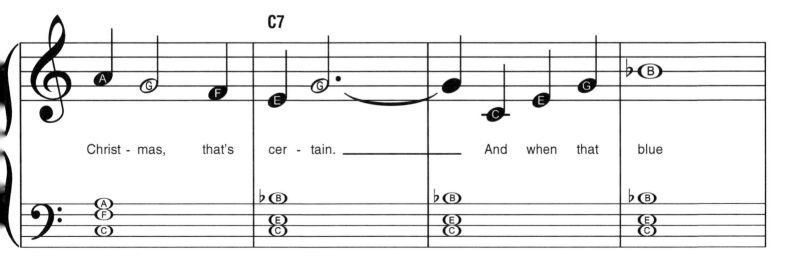

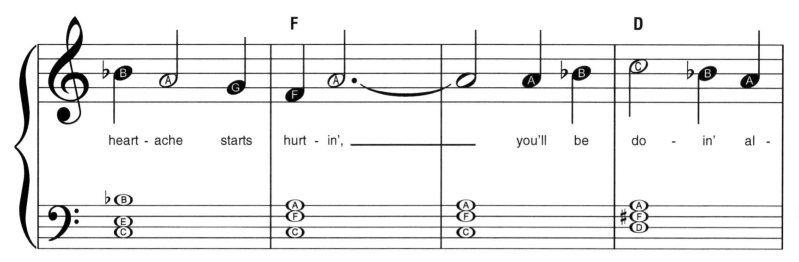

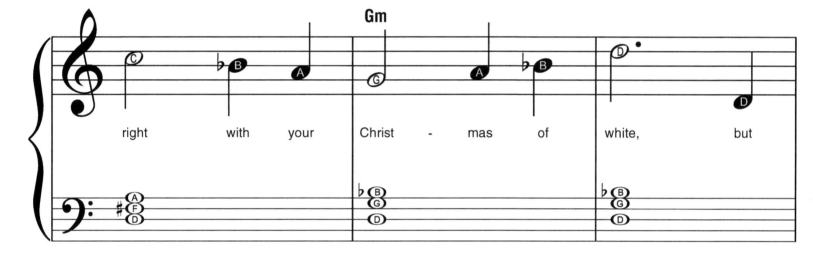

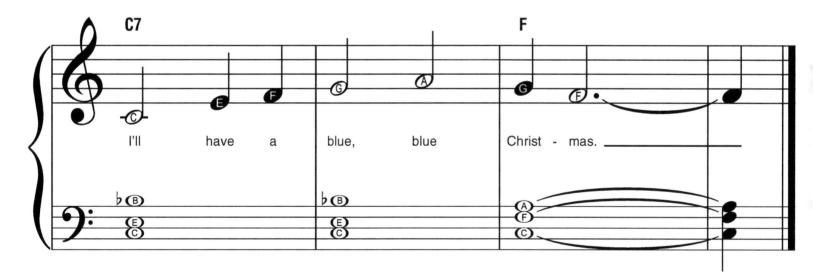

The Christmas Song
(Chestnuts Roasting on an Open Fire)

Music and Lyric by Mel Tormé
and Robert Wells

Moderately slow

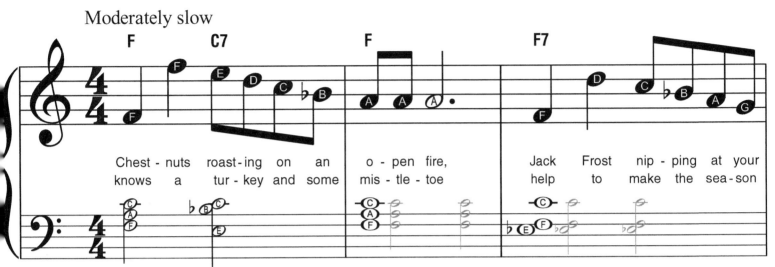

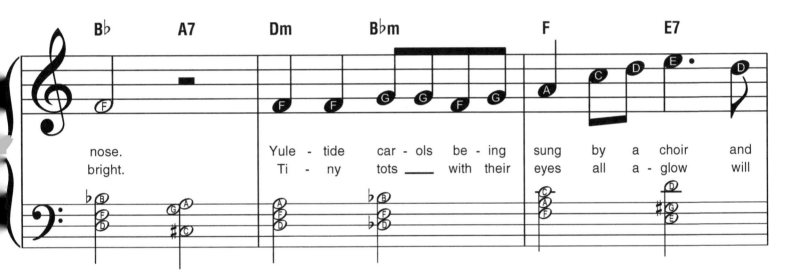

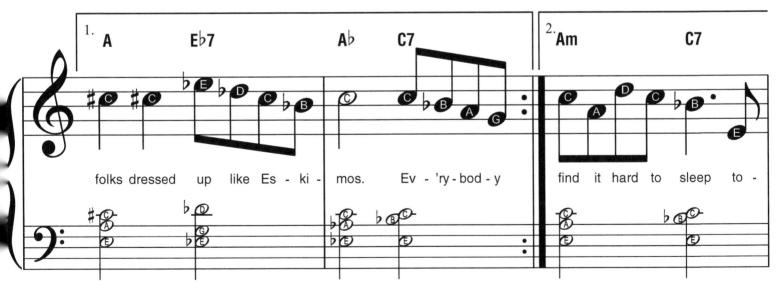

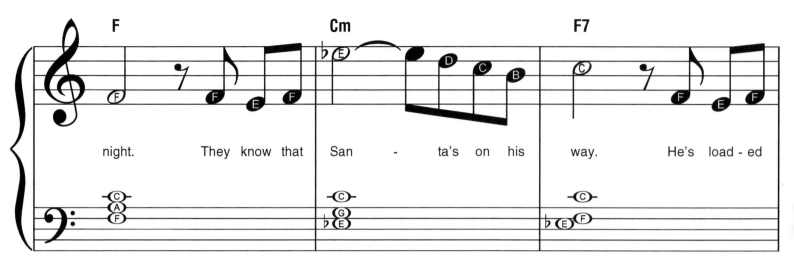

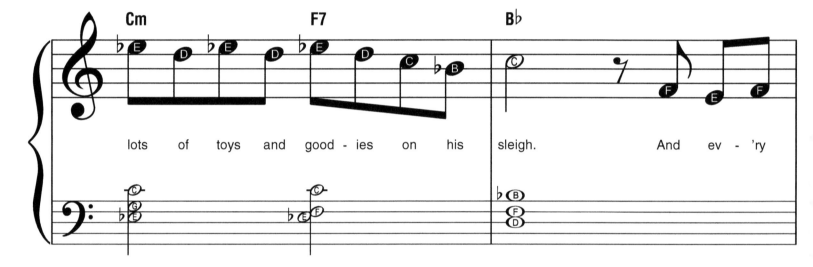

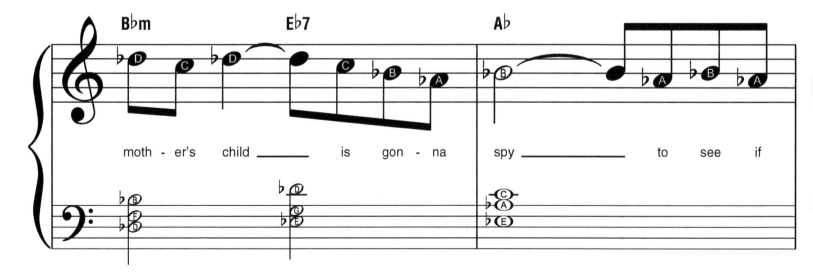

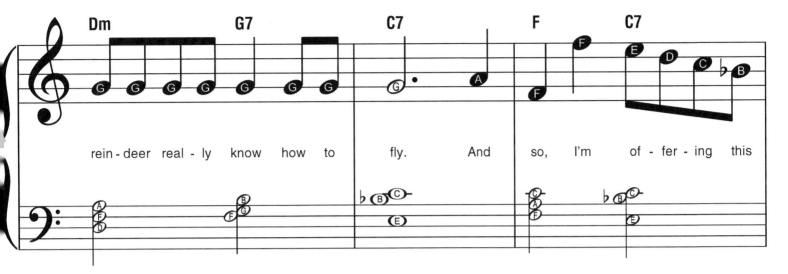

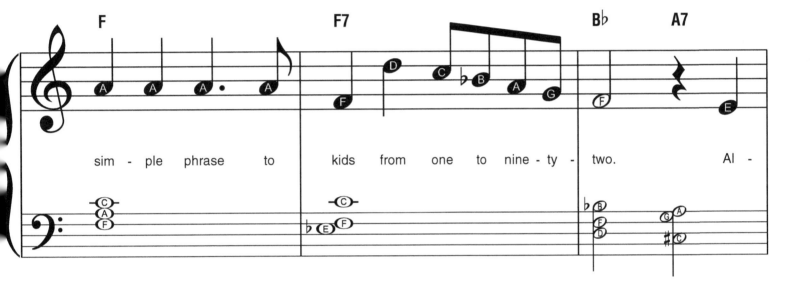

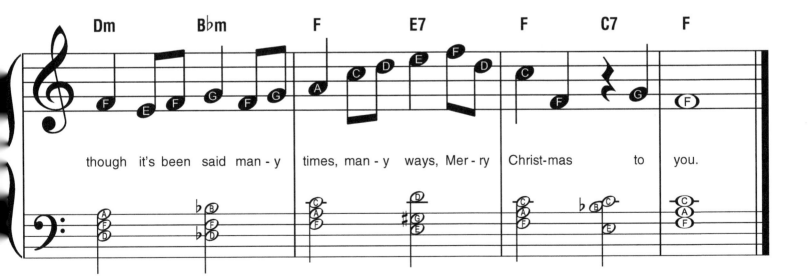

The Chipmunk Song

Words and Music by
Ross Bagdasarian

Moderate Waltz

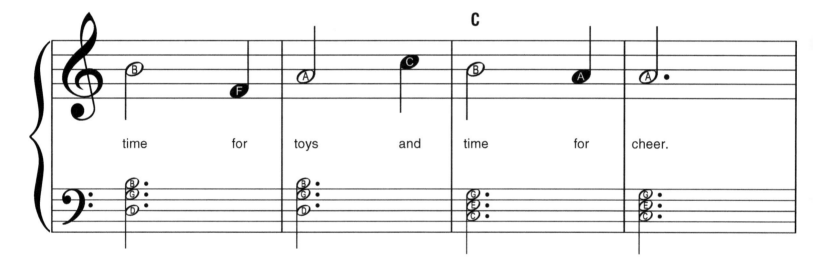

Christ - mas, Christ - mas time is near,

time for toys and time for cheer.

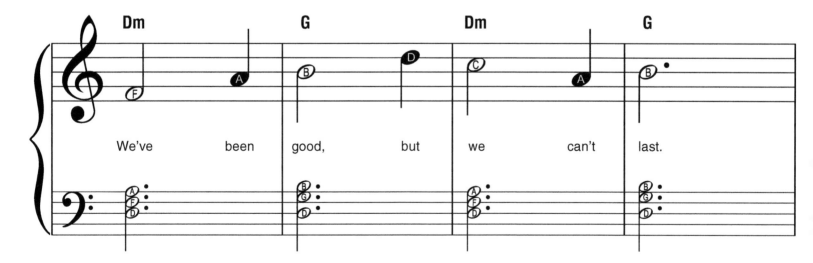

We've been good, but we can't last.

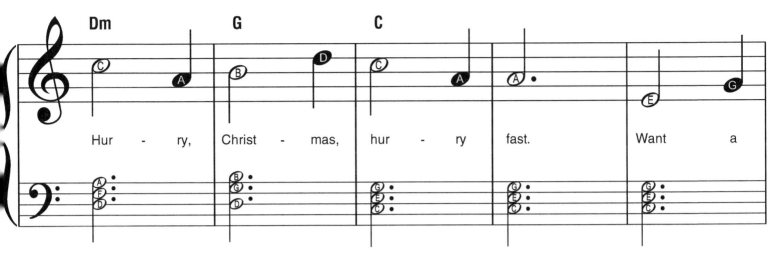

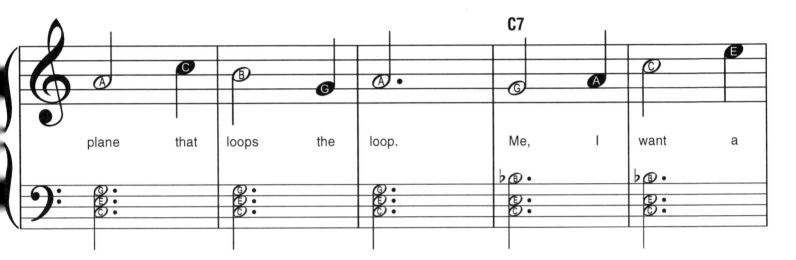

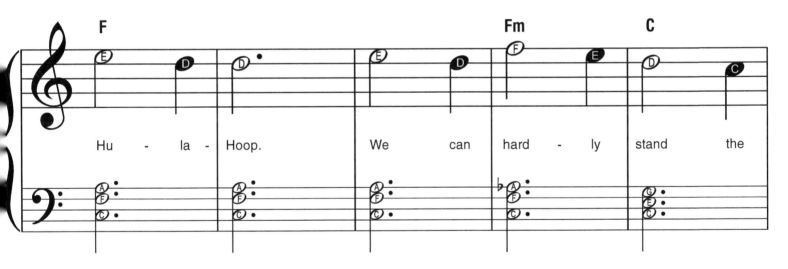

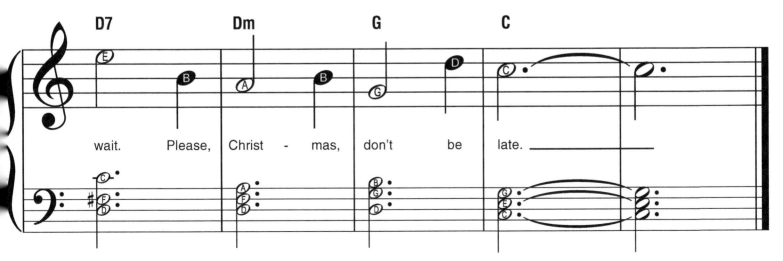

Christmas Time Is Here

from A CHARLIE BROWN CHRISTMAS

Words by Lee Mendelson
Music by Vince Guaraldi

Moderately

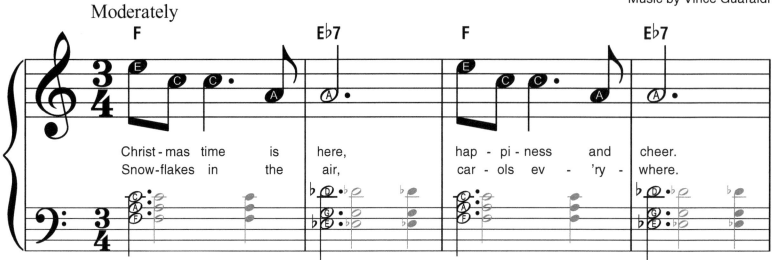

Christ-mas time   is   here,   hap - pi - ness   and   cheer.
Snow-flakes   in   the   air,   car - ols   ev - 'ry - where.

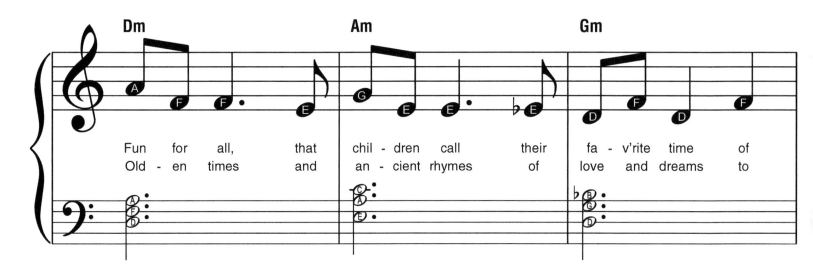

Fun   for   all,   that   chil - dren   call   their   fa - v'rite   time   of
Old - en   times   that   and   an - cient   rhymes   of   love   and   dreams   to

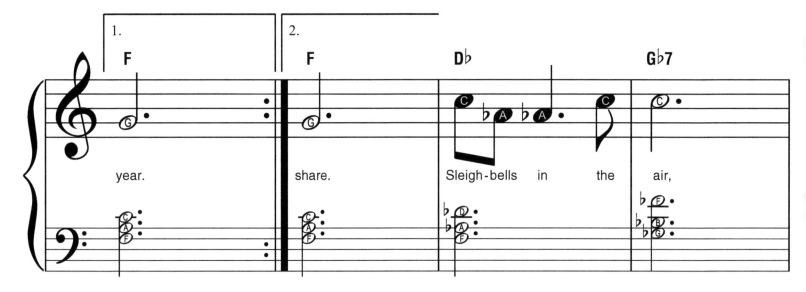

year.   share.   Sleigh-bells   in   the   air,

21

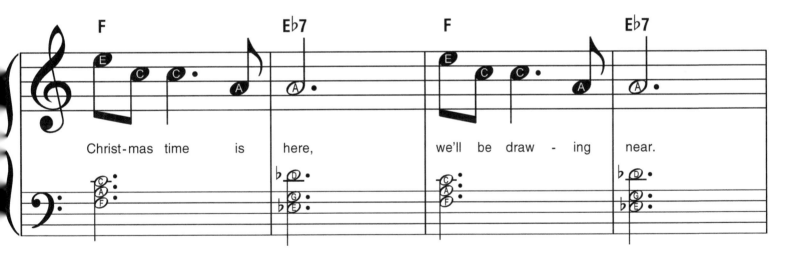

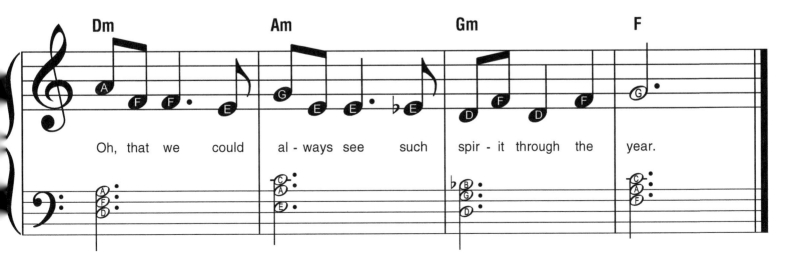

Do You Hear What I Hear

Words and Music by Noel Regney
and Gloria Shayne

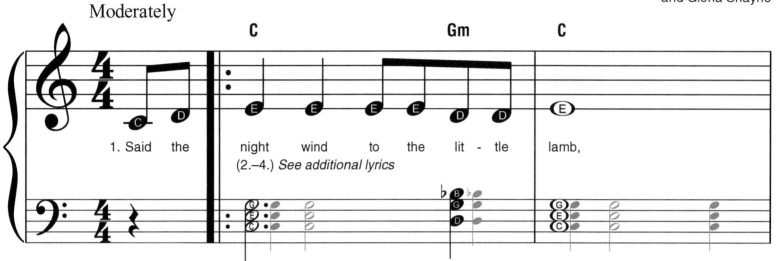

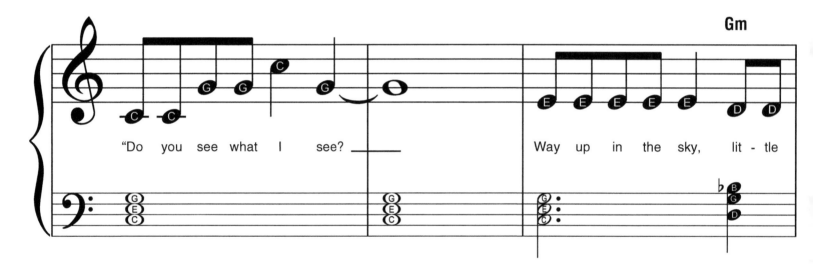

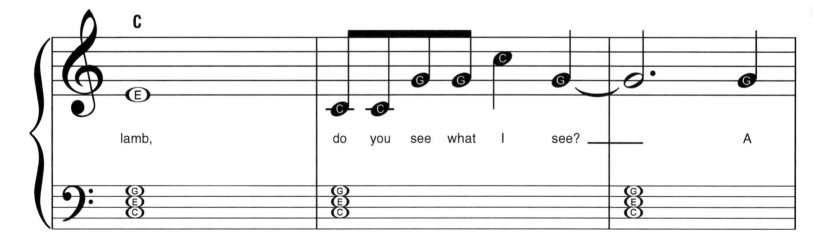

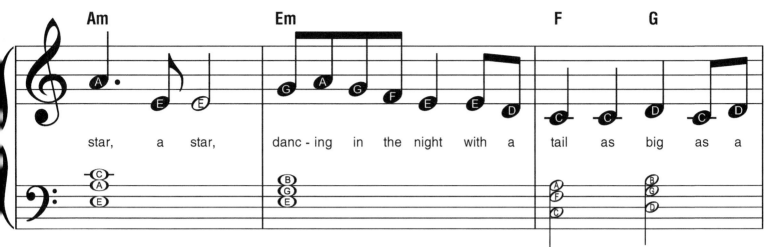
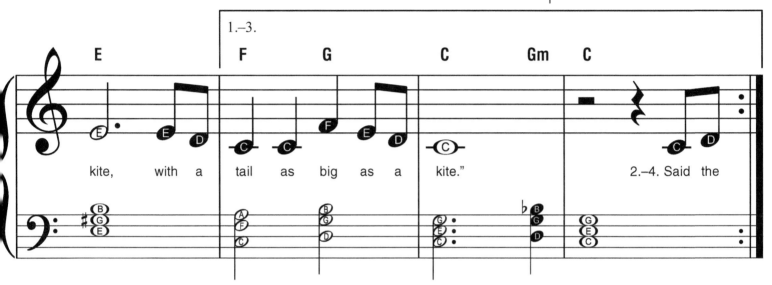
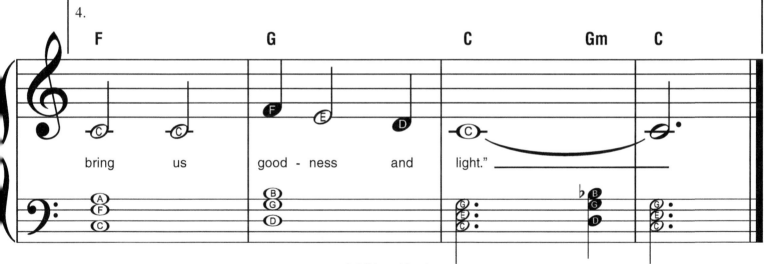

Additional Lyrics

2. Said the little lamb to the shepherd boy,
   "Do you hear what I hear?
   Ringing through the sky, shepherd boy,
   Do you hear what I hear?
   A song, a song, high above the tree,
   With a voice as big as the sea,
   With a voice as big as the sea."

3. Said the shepherd boy to the mighty king,
   "Do you know what I know?
   In your palace warm, mighty king,
   Do you know what I know?
   A Child, a Child shivers in the cold;
   Let us bring Him silver and gold,
   Let us bring Him silver and gold."

4. Said the king to the people everywhere,
   "Listen to what I say!
   Pray for peace, people everywhere.
   Listen to what I say!
   The Child, the Child, sleeping in the night,
   He will bring us goodness and light,
   He will bring us goodness and light."

Feliz Navidad

Music and Lyrics by
José Feliciano

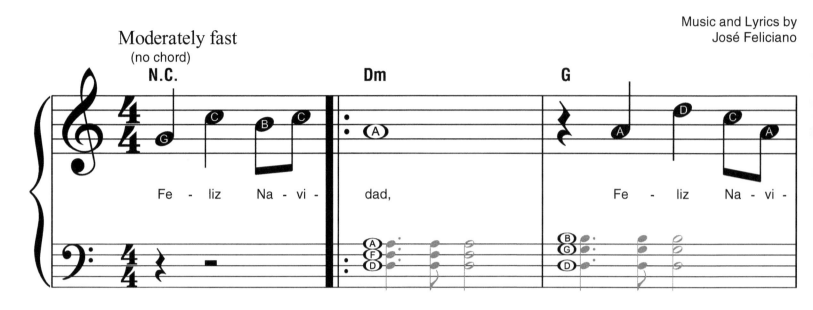

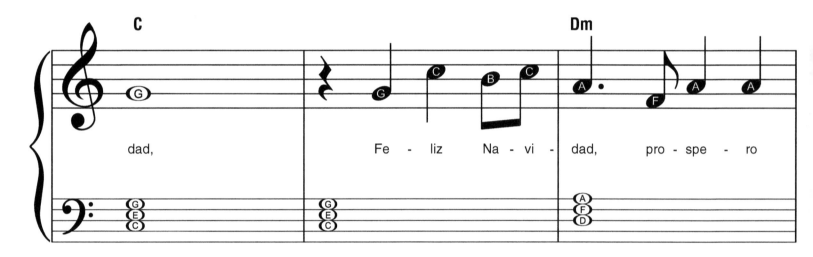

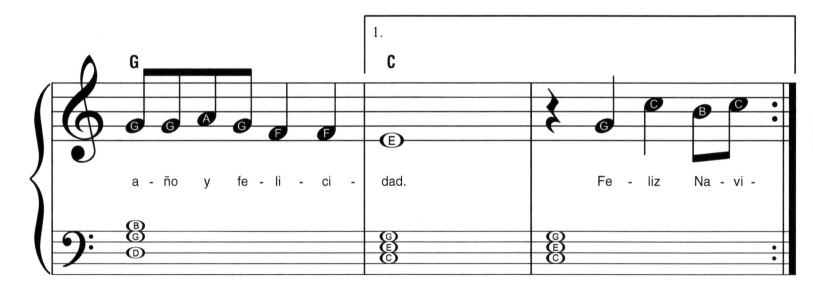

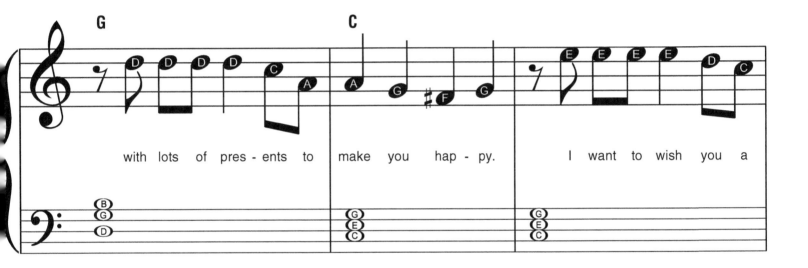

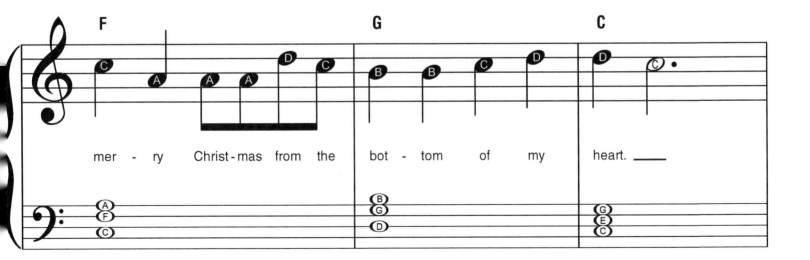

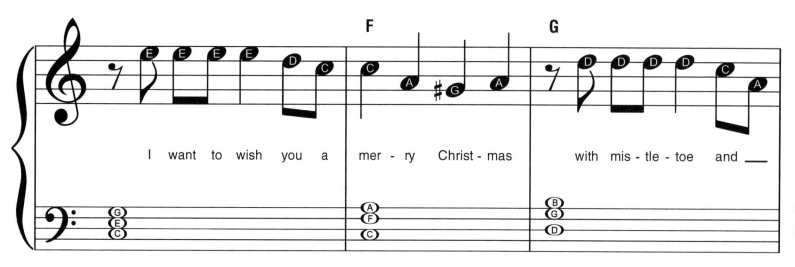

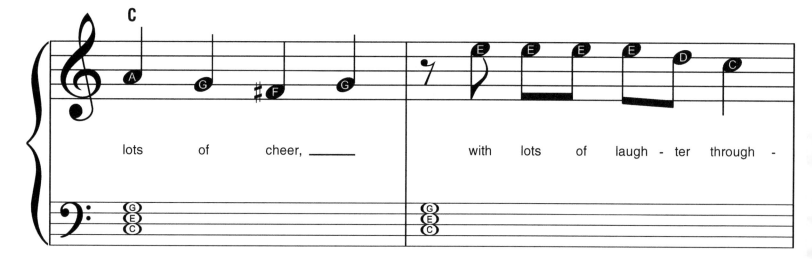

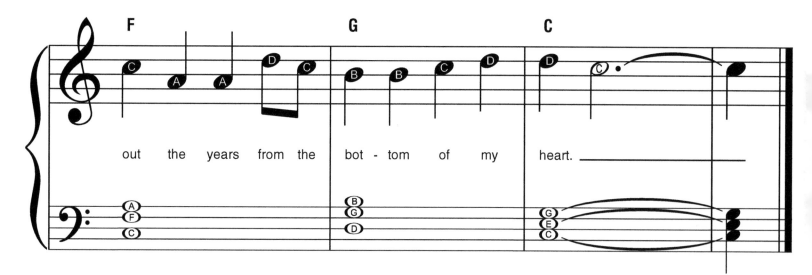

Frosty the Snow Man

Words and Music by Steve Nelson
and Jack Rollins

Moderately fast Shuffle

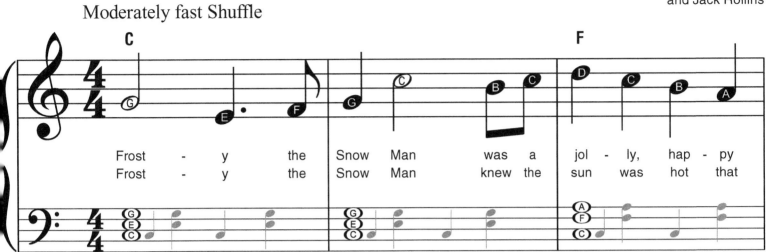

Frost - y the Snow Man was a jol - ly, hap - py
Frost - y the Snow Man knew the sun was hot that

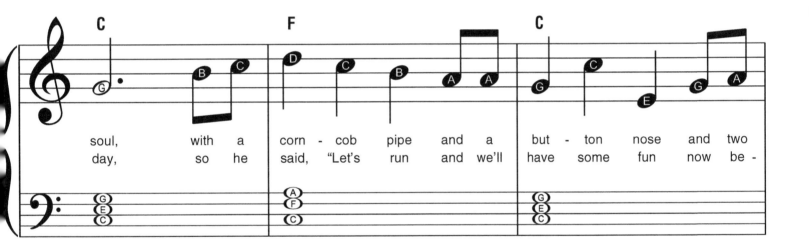

soul, with a corn - cob pipe and a but - ton nose and two
day, so he said, "Let's run and we'll have some fun now be -

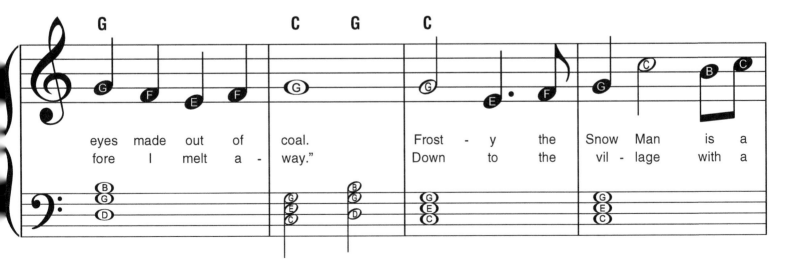

eyes made out of coal. Frost - y the Snow Man is a
fore I melt a - way." Down to the vil - lage with a

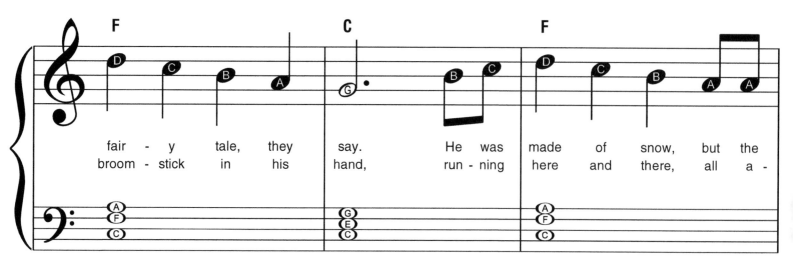

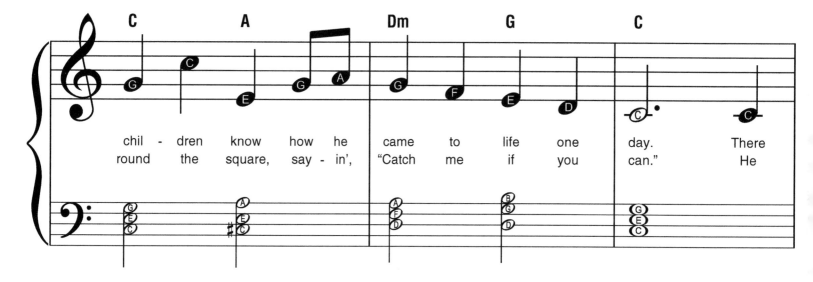

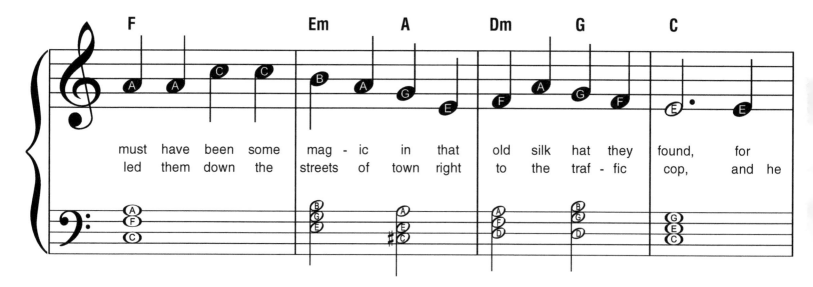

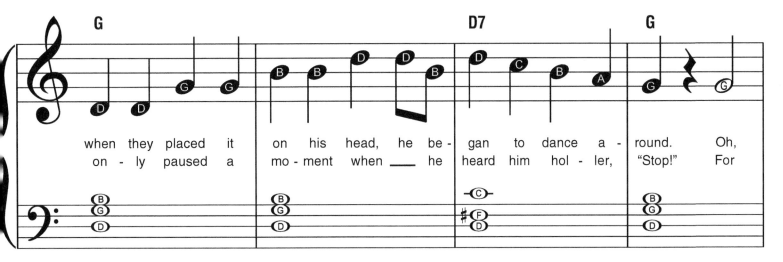

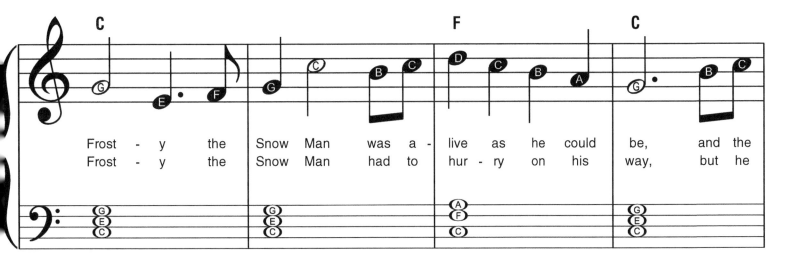

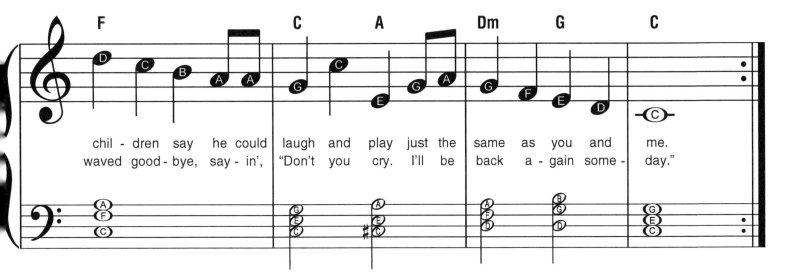

Grown-Up Christmas List

Words and Music by David Foster
and Linda Thompson-Jenner

Moderately slow

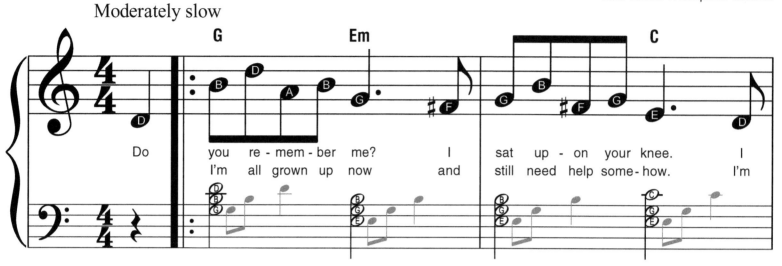

Do you re-mem-ber me? I sat up-on your knee. I
I'm all grown up now and still need help some-how. I'm

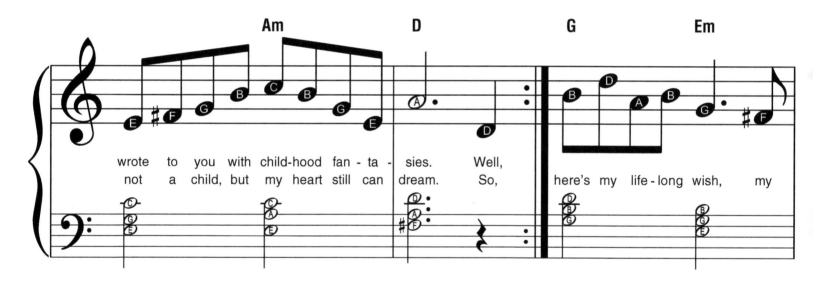

wrote to you with child-hood fan-ta - sies. Well,
not a child, but my heart still can dream. So,

here's my life-long wish, my

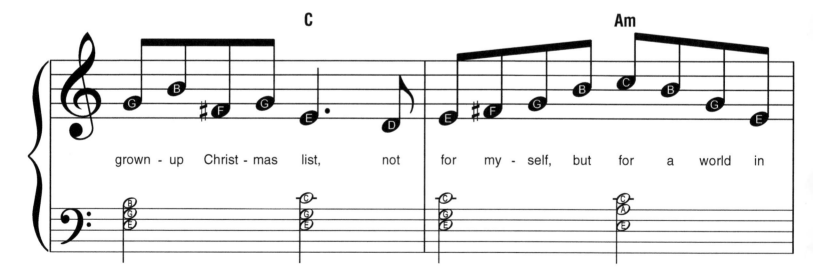

grown-up Christ-mas list, not for my-self, but for a world in

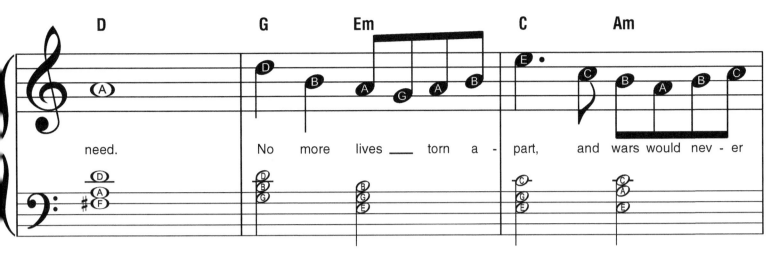

need.   No more lives ___ torn a - part,   and wars would nev - er

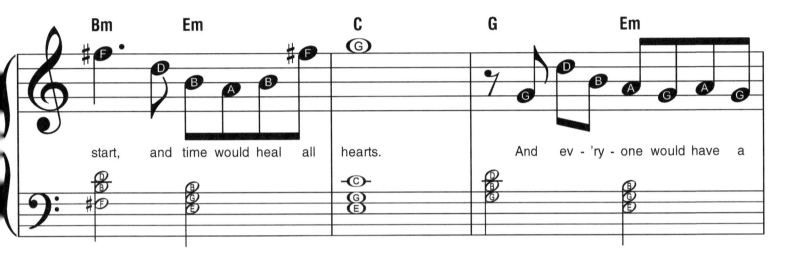

start,   and time would heal all   hearts.   And   ev - 'ry - one would have   a

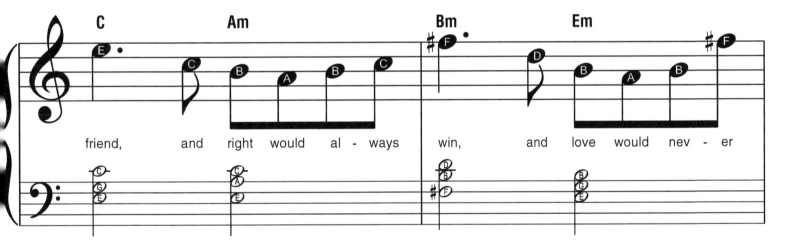

friend,   and right would al - ways   win,   and love would nev - er

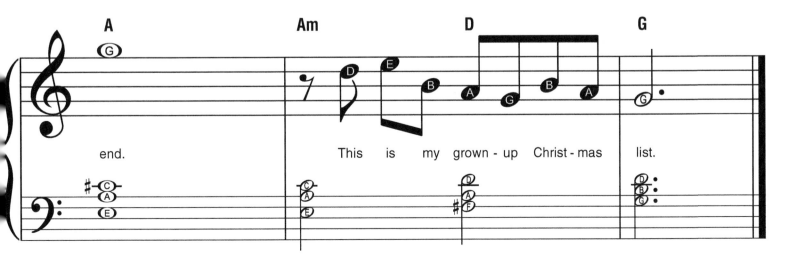

end.   This   is   my grown - up Christ - mas   list.

Have Yourself a Merry Little Christmas

from MEET ME IN ST. LOUIS

Words and Music by Hugh Martin
and Ralph Blane

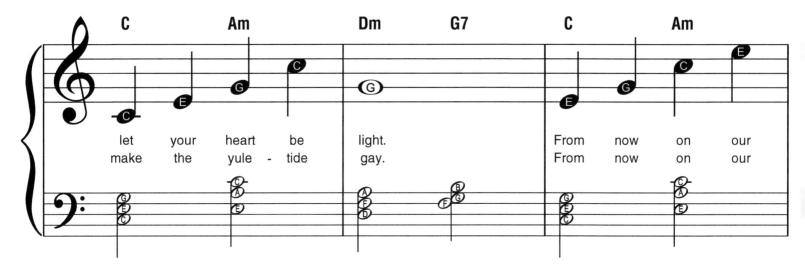

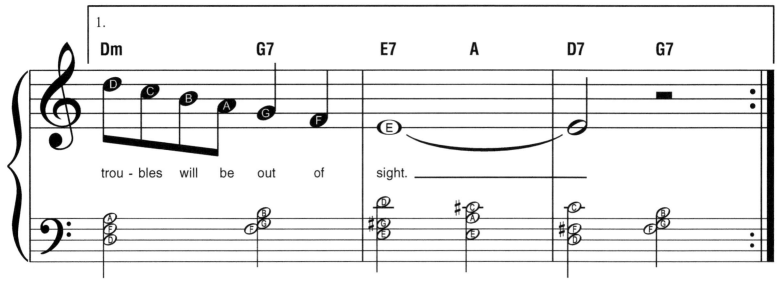

33

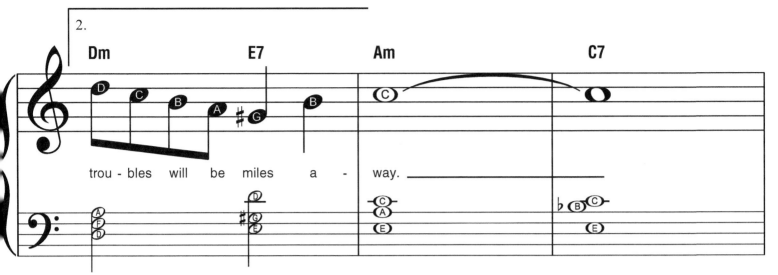

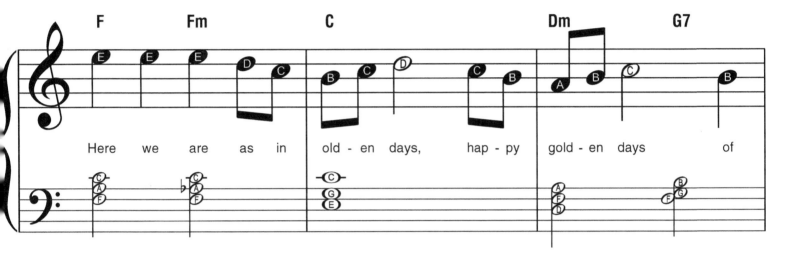

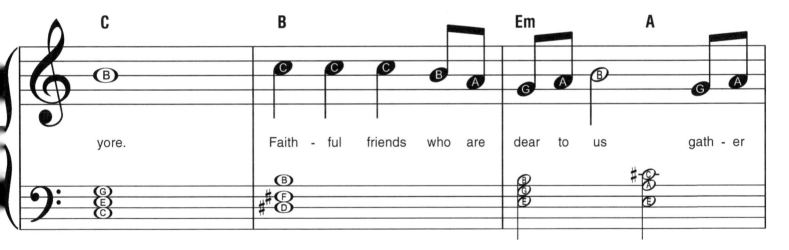

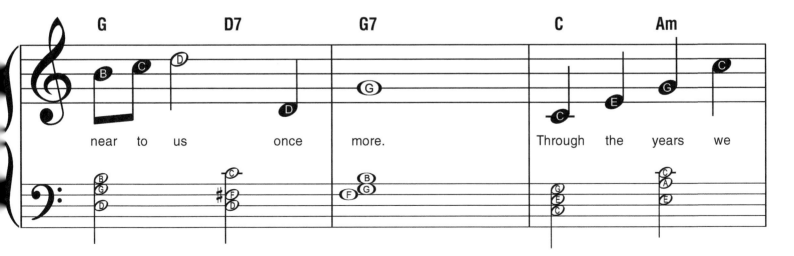

34

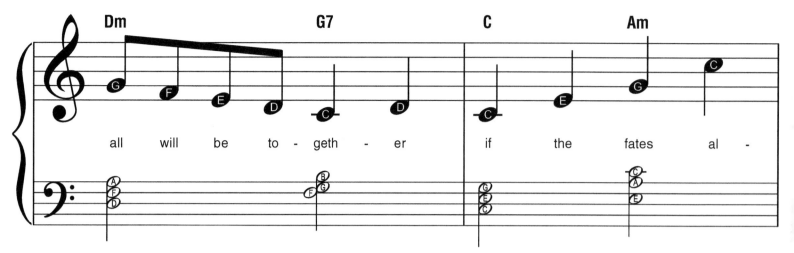

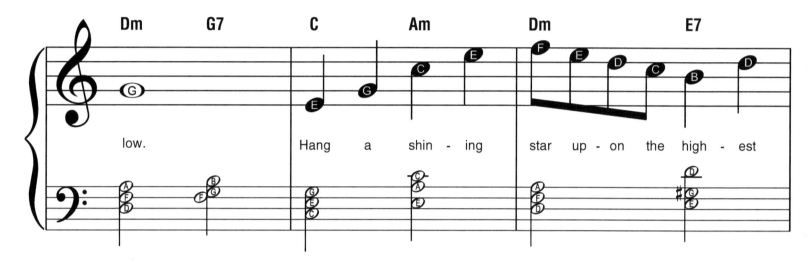

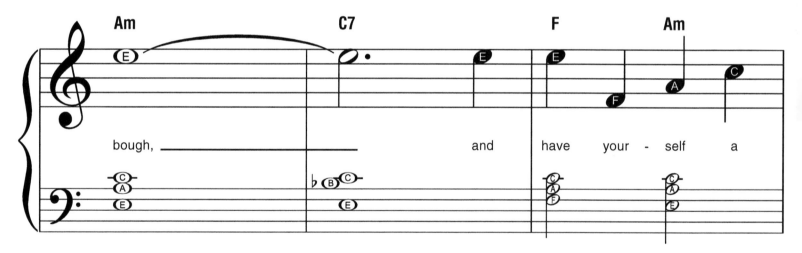

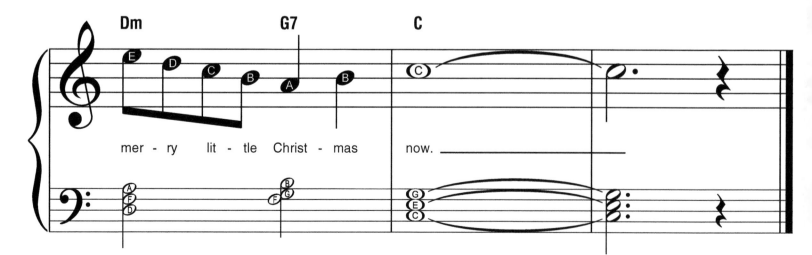

(There's No Place Like)
Home for the Holidays

Words and Music by Al Stillman
and Robert Allen

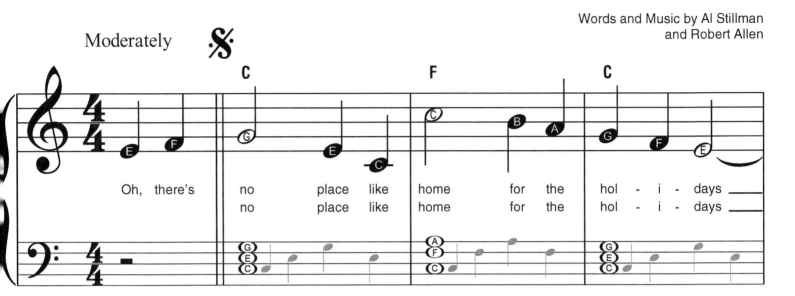

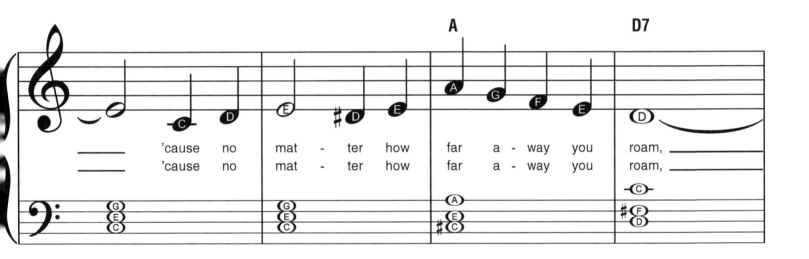

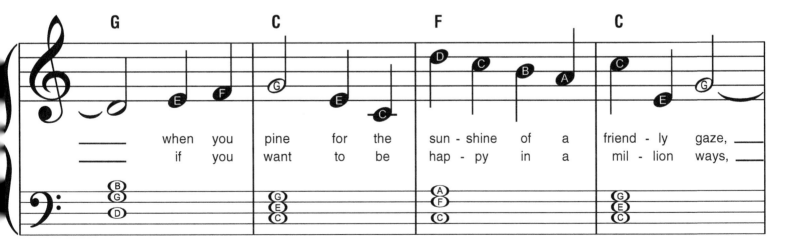

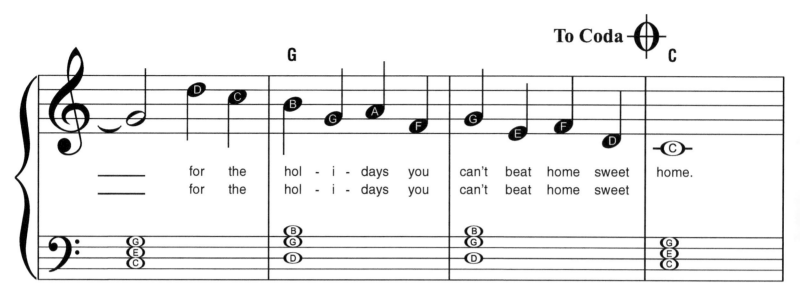

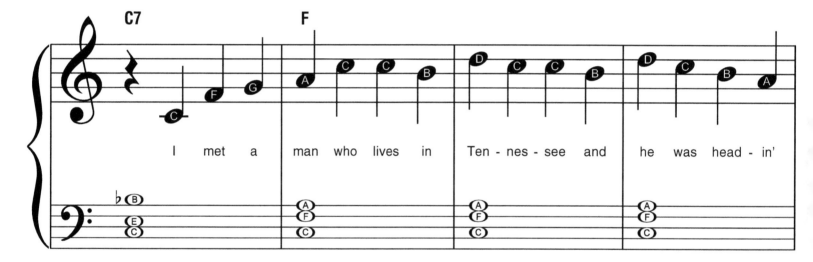

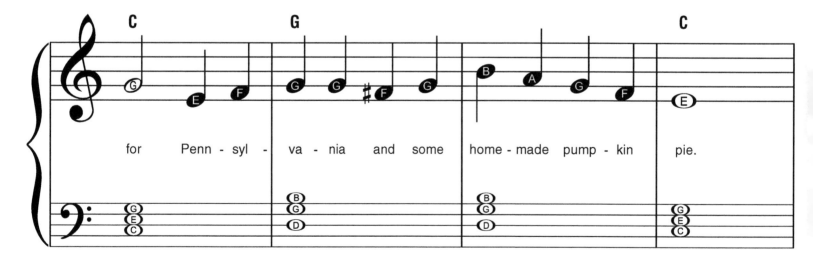

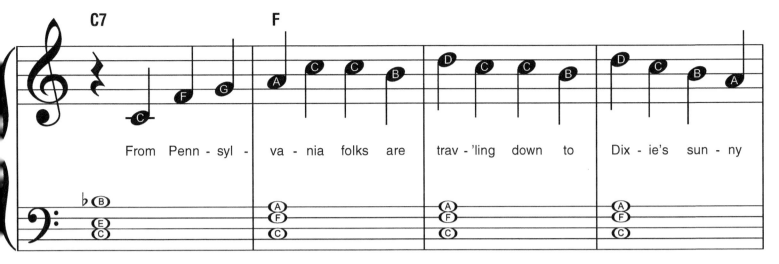

From Penn - syl - va - nia folks are trav - 'ling down to Dix - ie's sun - ny

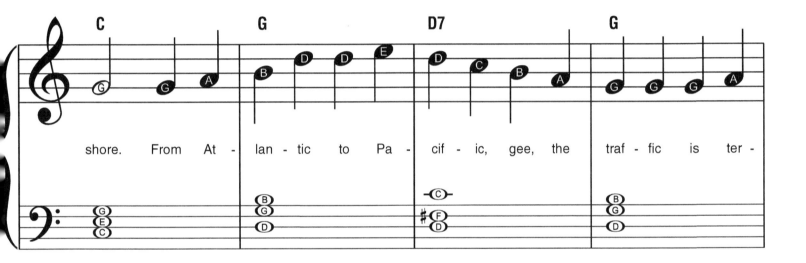

shore. From At - lan - tic to Pa - cif - ic, gee, the traf - fic is ter -

D.S. al Coda

(Return to 𝄋, play to ⊕
and skip to Coda)

CODA

rif - ic! Oh, there's

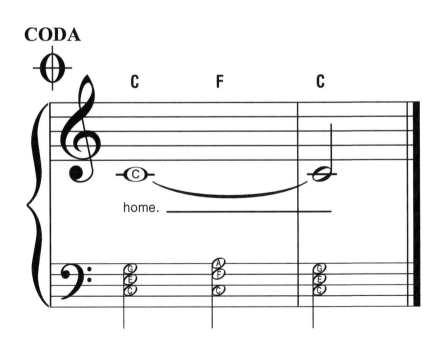

home. _____

Here Comes Santa Claus
(Right Down Santa Claus Lane)

Words and Music by Gene Autry
and Oakley Haldeman

Bright Shuffle

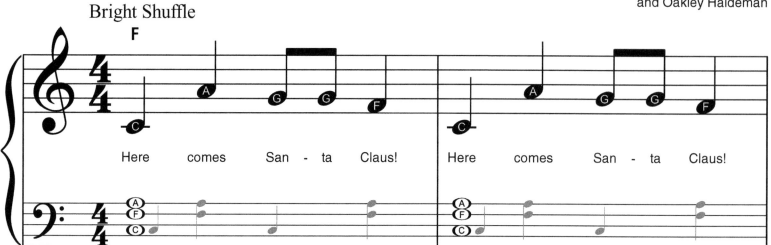

Here comes San - ta Claus! Here comes San - ta Claus!

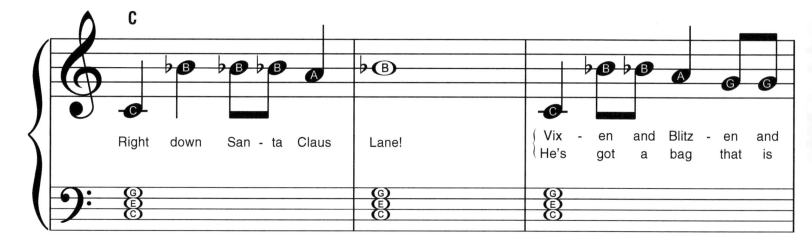

Right down San - ta Claus Lane!

{ Vix - en and Blitz - en and
{ He's got a bag that is

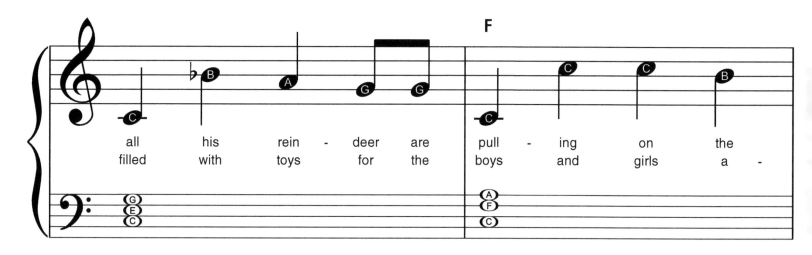

all his rein - deer are pull - ing on the
filled with toys for the boys and girls a -

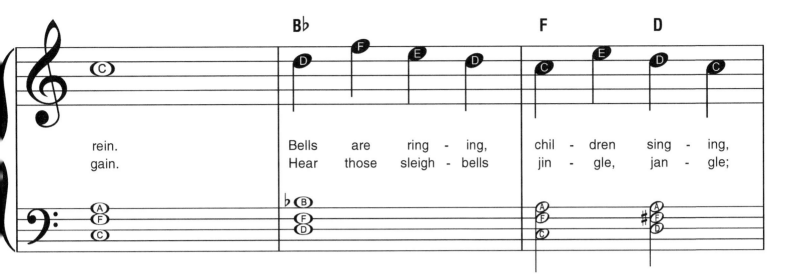

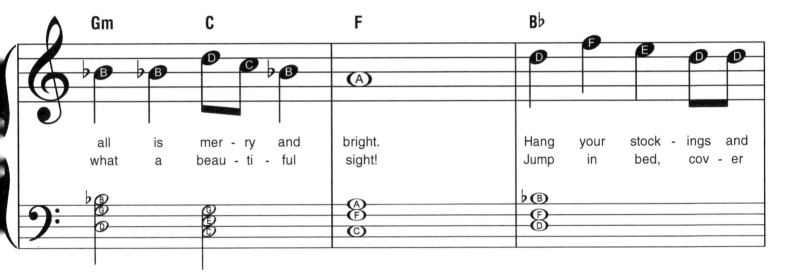

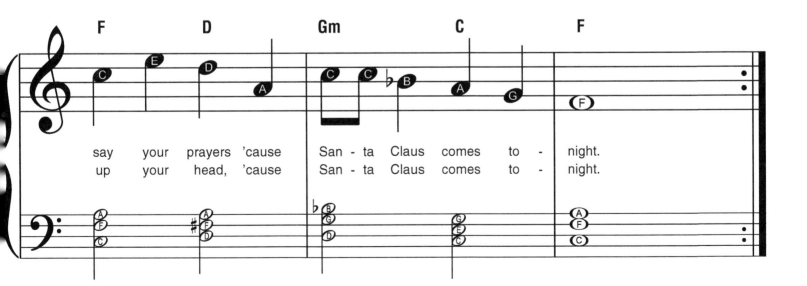

A Holly Jolly Christmas

Music and Lyrics by
Johnny Marks

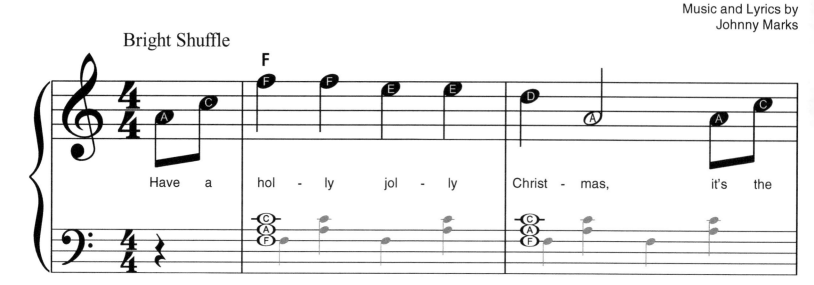

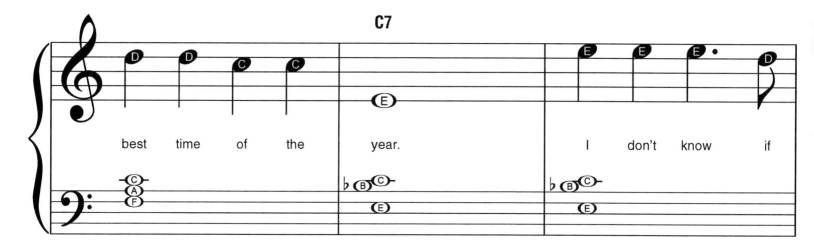

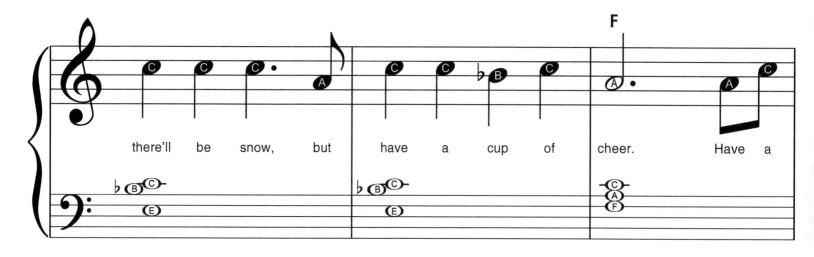

41

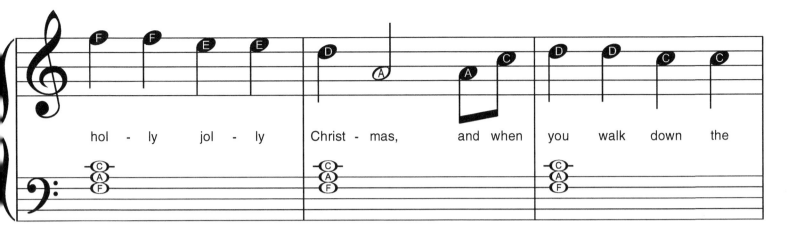

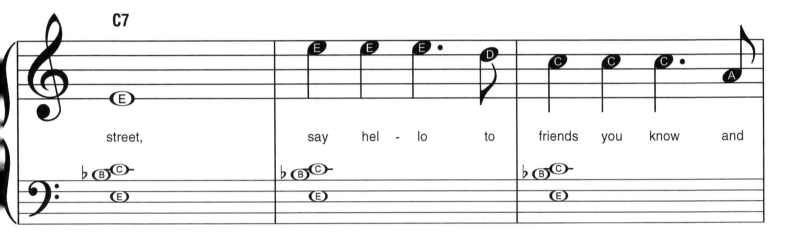

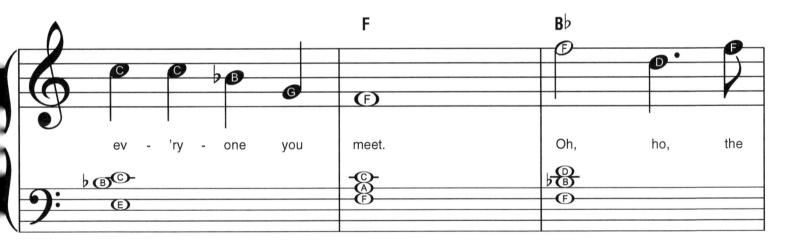

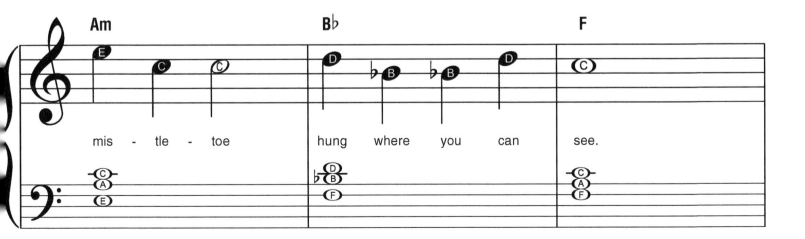

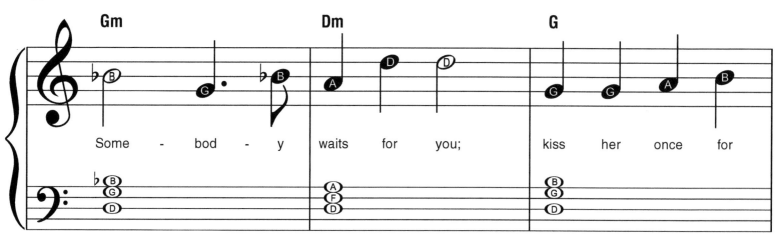

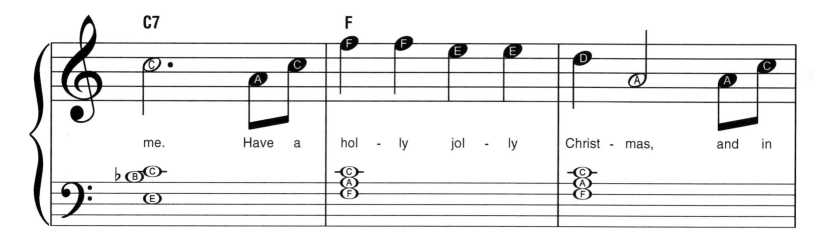

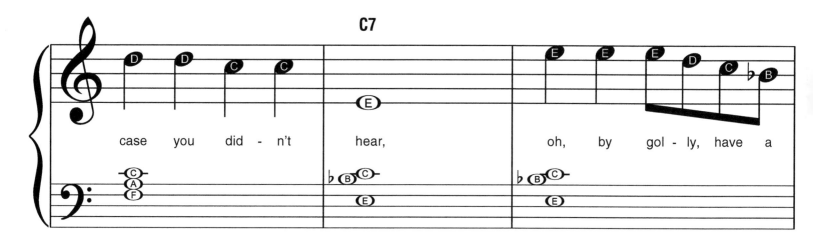

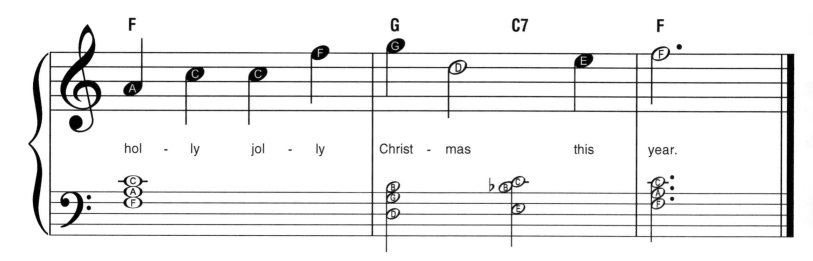

It's Beginning to
Look Like Christmas

By Meredith Willson

Moderate Shuffle

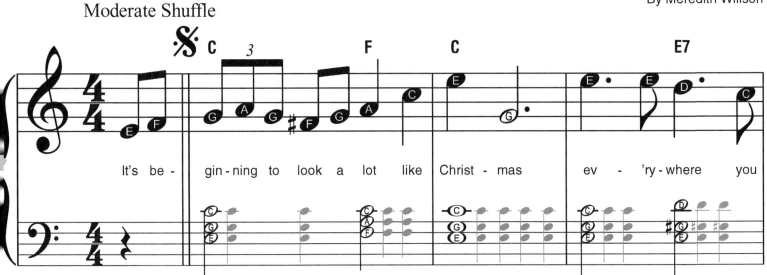

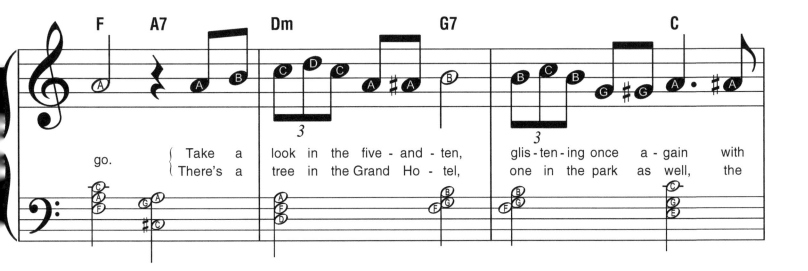

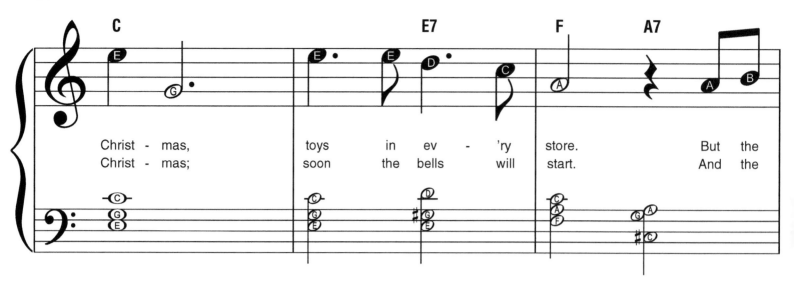

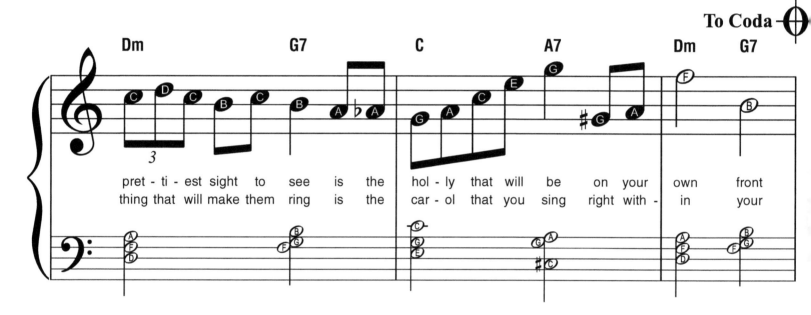

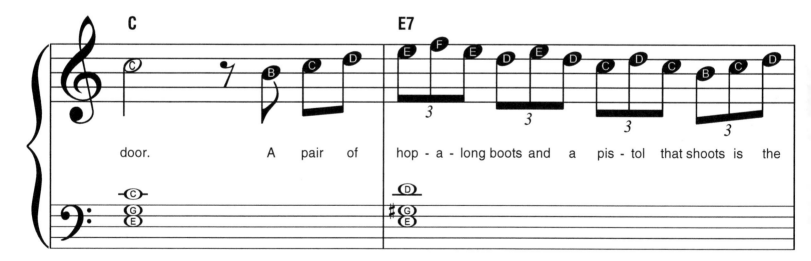

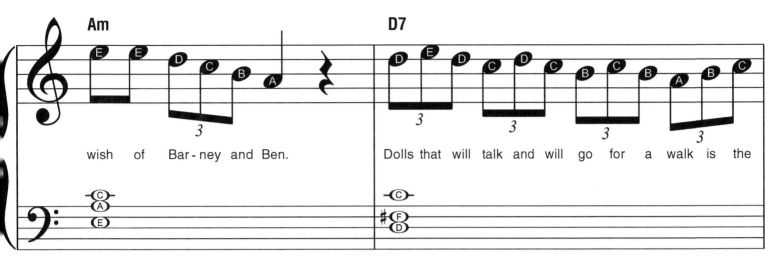

Am — wish of Bar - ney and Ben. **D7** — Dolls that will talk and will go for a walk is the

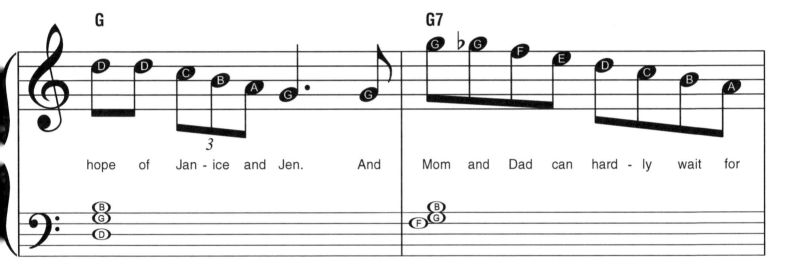

G — hope of Jan - ice and Jen. And **G7** — Mom and Dad can hard - ly wait for

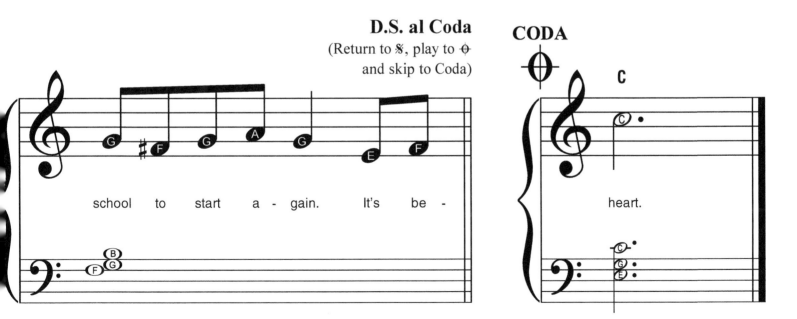

D.S. al Coda
(Return to 𝄋, play to ⊕
and skip to Coda)

school to start a - gain. It's be -

CODA

C — heart.

I Heard the Bells on Christmas Day

Words by Henry Wadsworth Longfellow
Adapted by Johnny Marks
Music by Johnny Marks

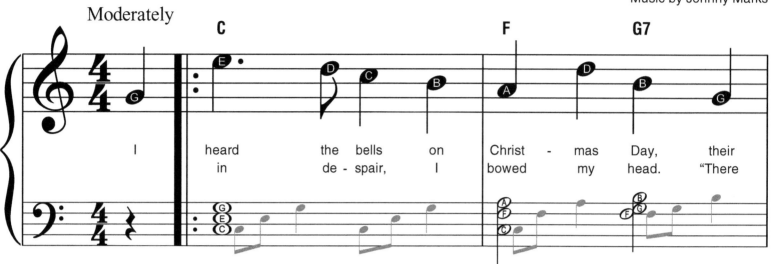

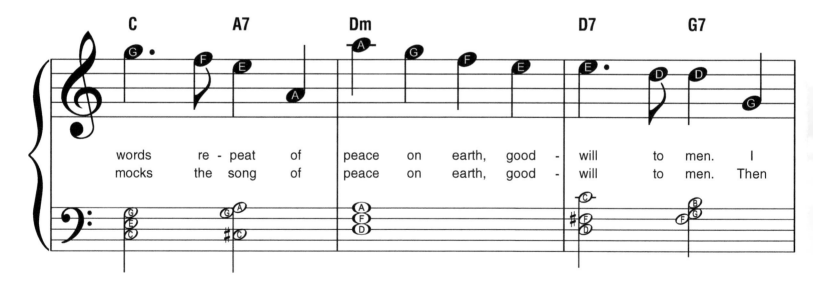

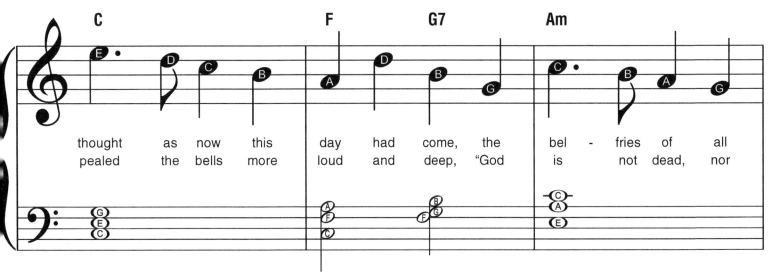

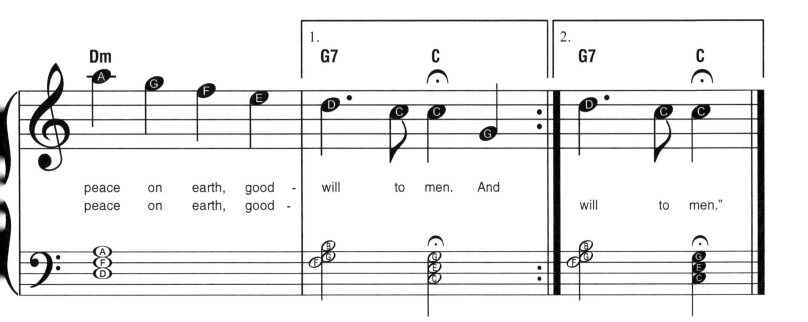

I'll Be Home for Christmas

Words and Music by Kim Gannon
and Walter Kent

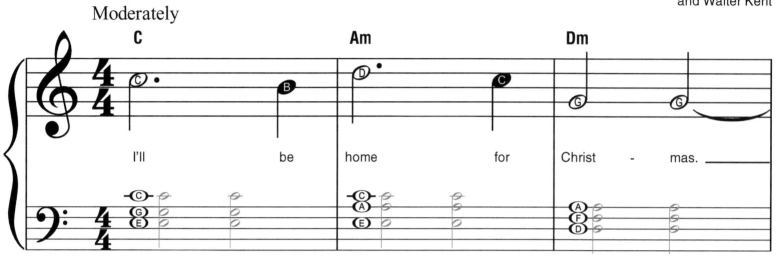

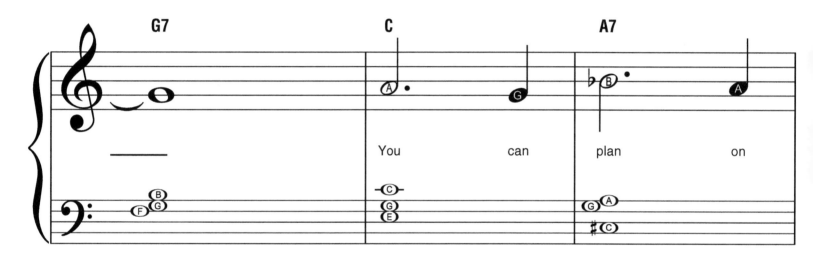

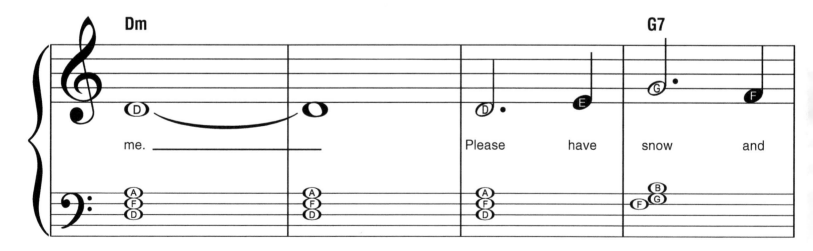

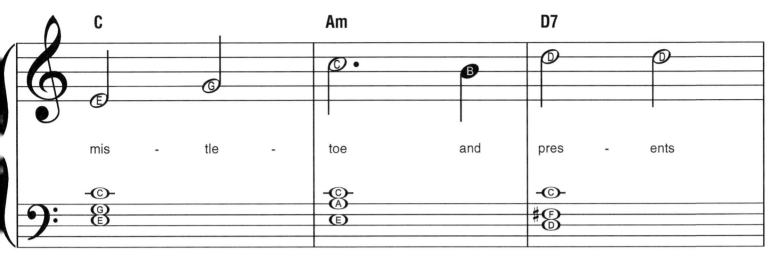

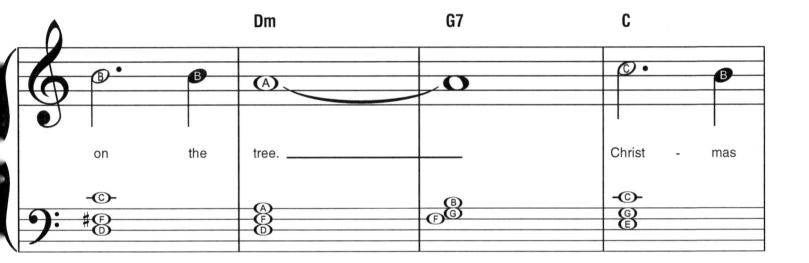

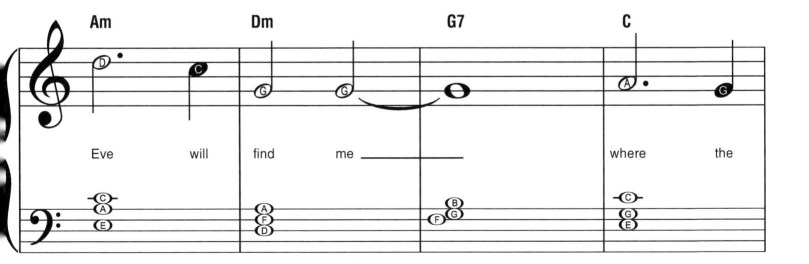

A7   **Dm**

love - light   gleams. _____   I'll   be

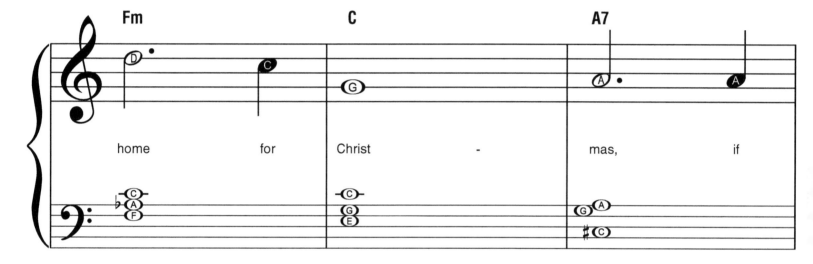

Fm   **C**   **A7**

home   for   Christ - mas,   if

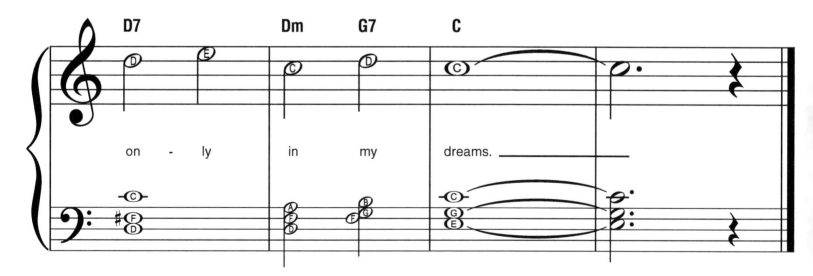

D7   **Dm**   **G7**   **C**

on - ly   in   my   dreams. _____

Jingle Bell Rock

Words and Music by Joe Beal
and Jim Boothe

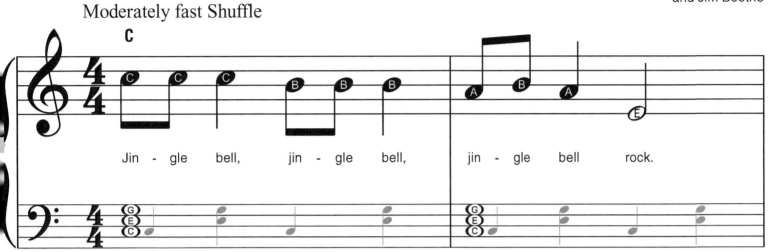

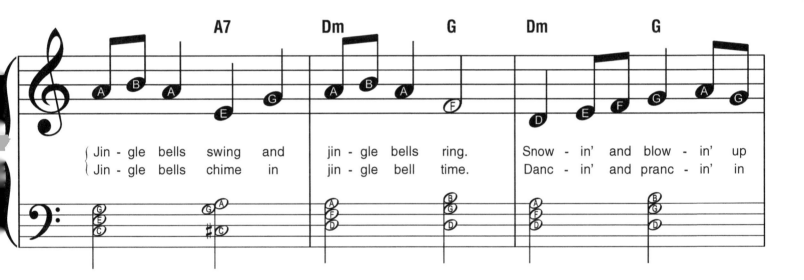

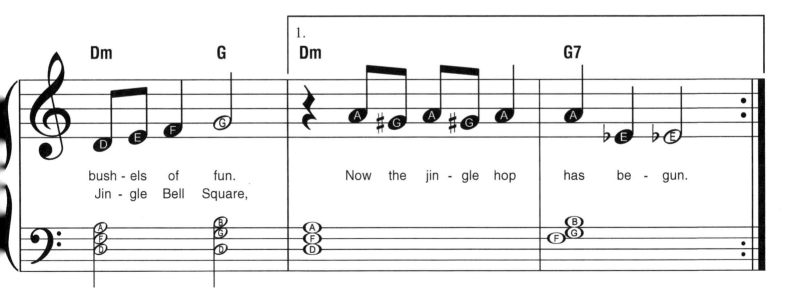

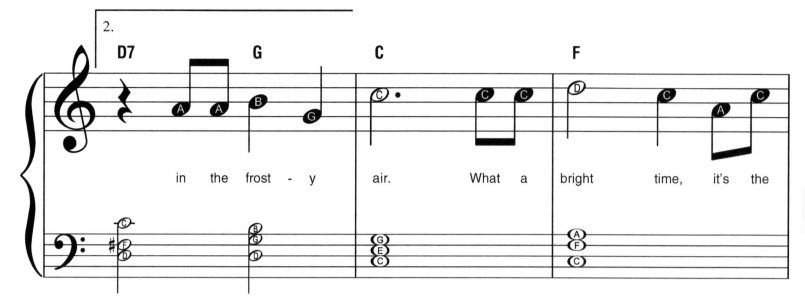

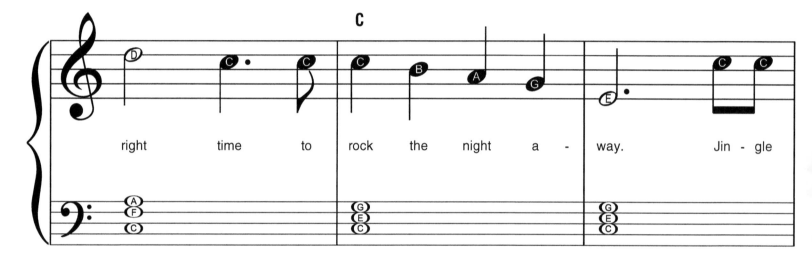

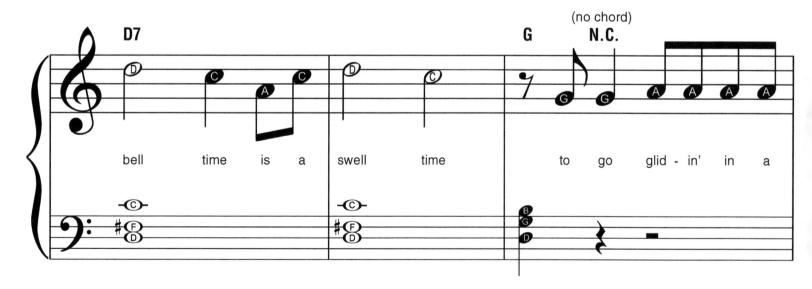

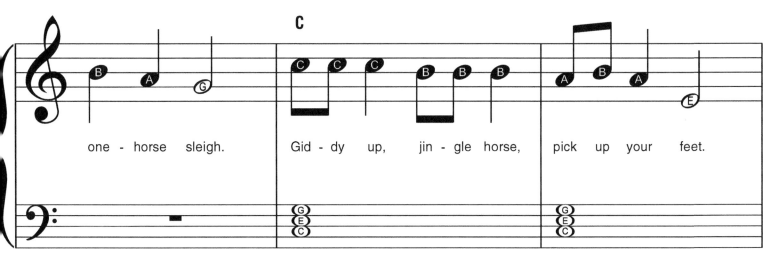

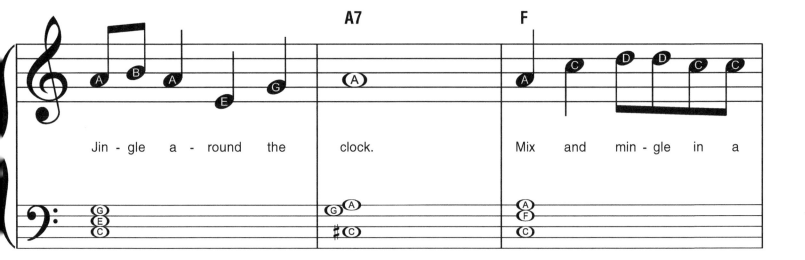

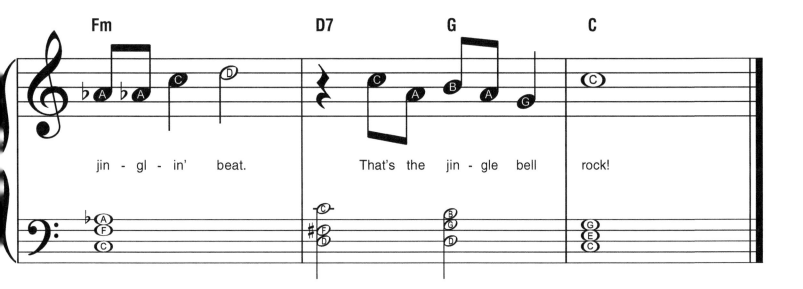

The Little Drummer Boy

Words and Music by Harry Simeone,
Henry Onorati and Katherine Davis

Steady March

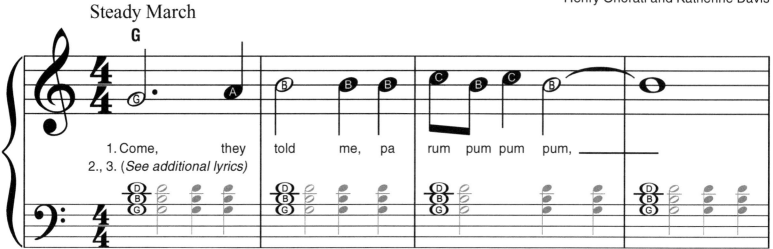

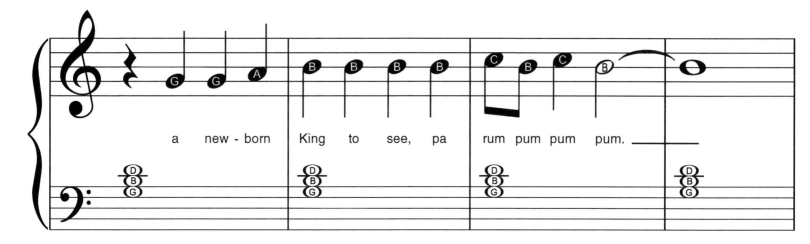

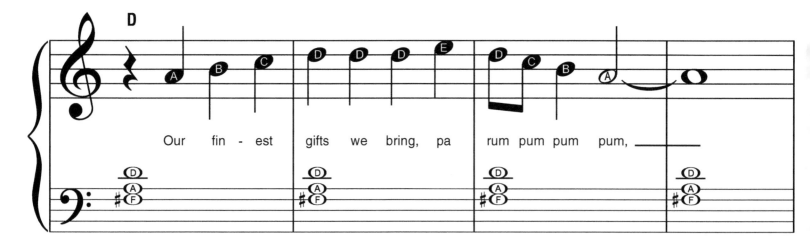

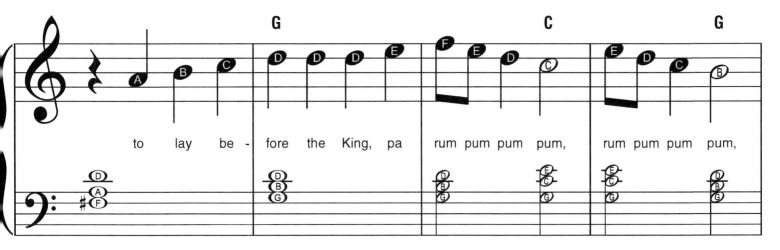

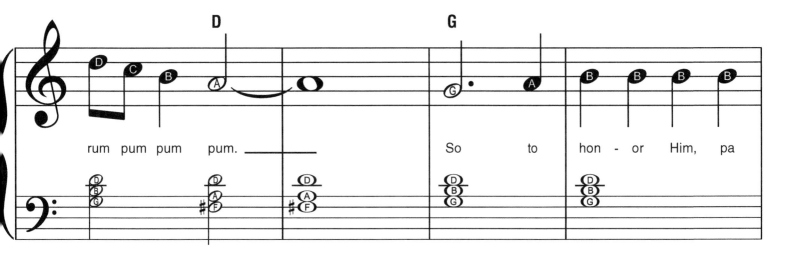

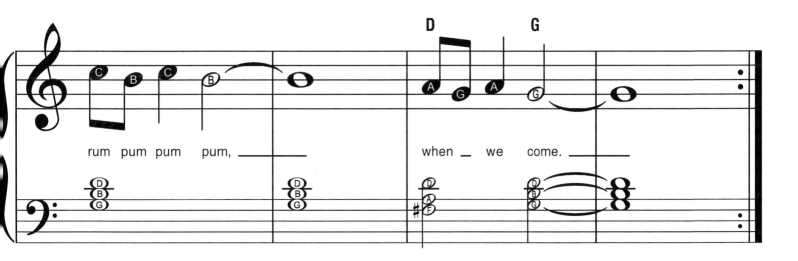

Additional Lyrics

2. Little baby, pa rum pum pum pum,
I am a poor boy, too, pa rum pum pum pum.
I have no gift to bring, pa rum pum pum pum,
That's fit to give our King, pa rum pum pum pum,
Rum pum pum pum, rum pum pum pum.
Shall I play for you, pa rum pum pum pum,
On my drum?

3. Mary nodded, pa rum pum pum pum,
The ox and lamb kept time, pa rum pum pum pum.
I played my drum for Him, pa rum pum pum pum,
I played my best for Him, pa rum pum pum pum,
Rum pum pum pum, rum pum pum pum.
Then He smiled at me, pa rum pum pum pum,
Me and my drum.

Little Saint Nick

Words and Music by Brian Wilson
and Mike Love

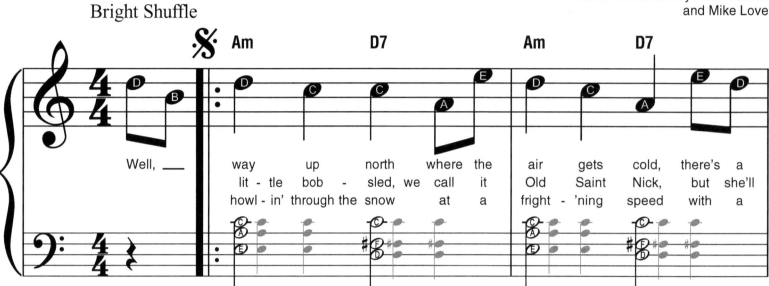

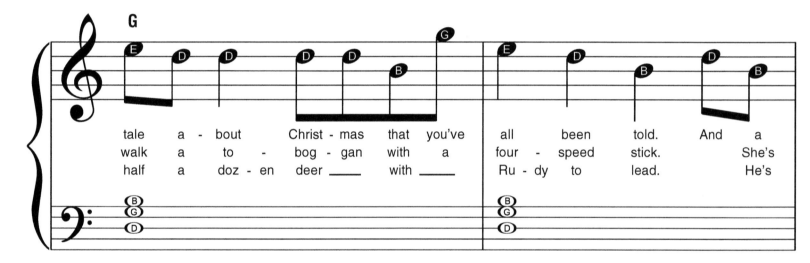

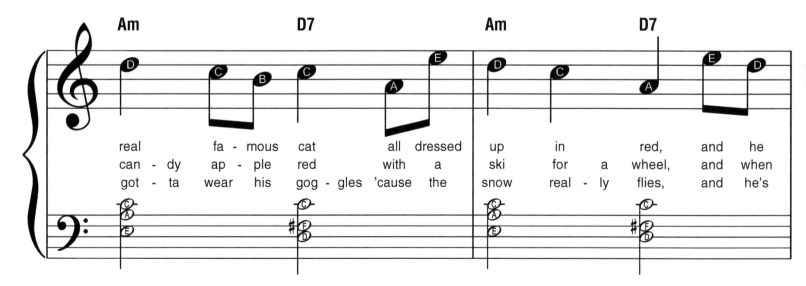

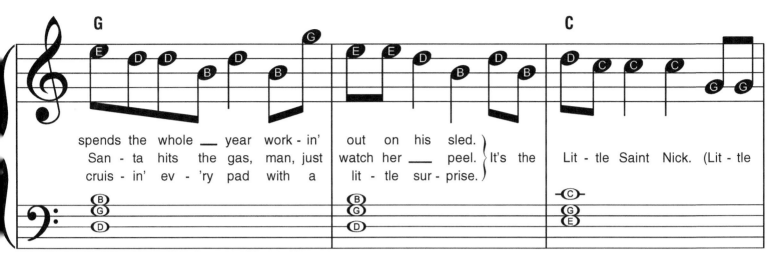

spends the whole ___ year work - in'
San - ta hits the gas, man, just
cruis - in' ev - 'ry pad with a

out on his sled.
watch her ___ peel.
lit - tle sur - prise.

It's the

Lit - tle Saint Nick. (Lit - tle

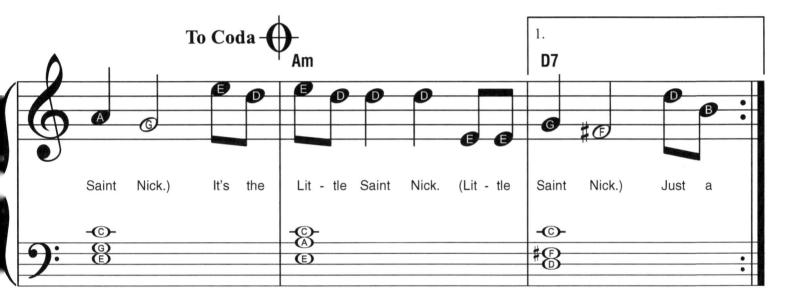

Saint Nick.)   It's the

Lit - tle Saint Nick. (Lit - tle

Saint Nick.)   Just a

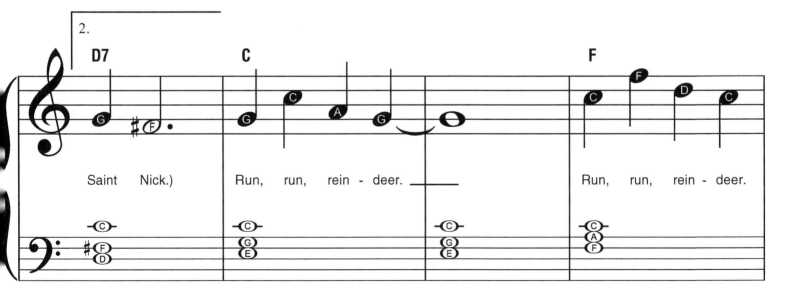

Saint Nick.)

Run, run, rein - deer. ___

Run, run, rein - deer.

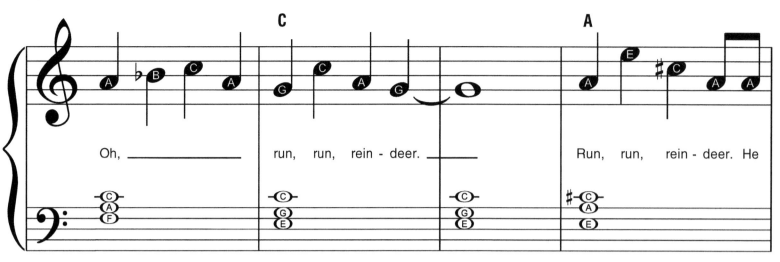

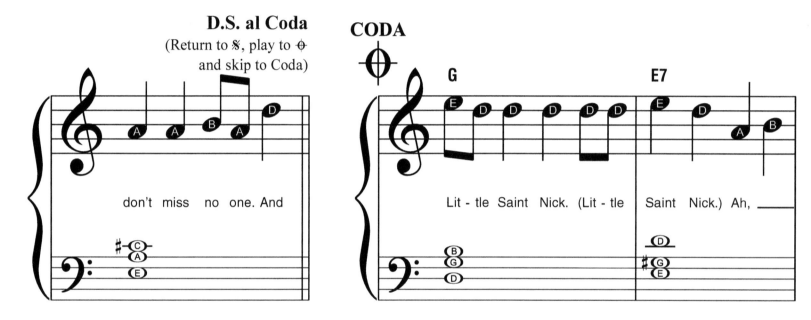

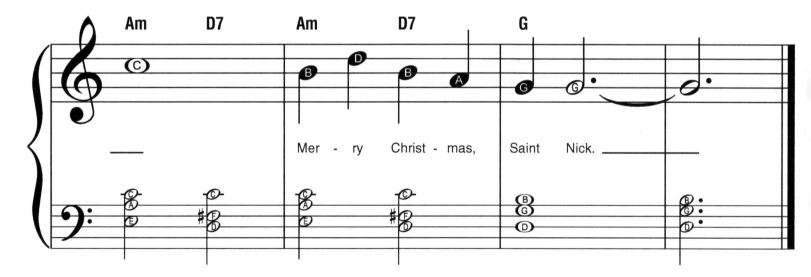

Let It Snow!
Let It Snow! Let It Snow!

Words by Sammy Cahn
Music by Jule Styne

Bright Shuffle

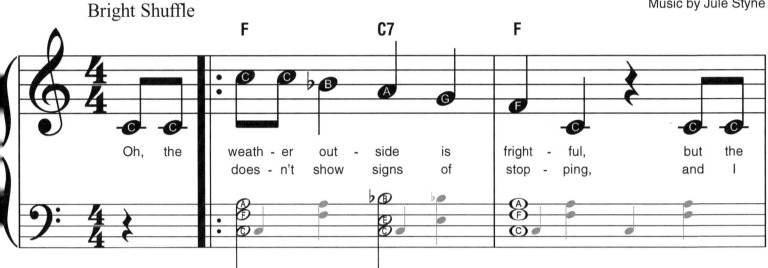

Oh, the weath-er out-side is fright-ful, but the
does-n't show signs of stop-ping, and I

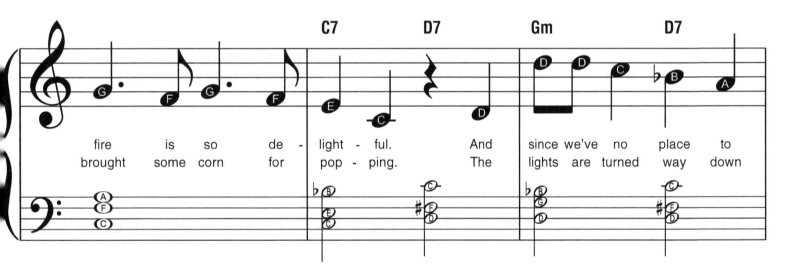

fire is so de-light-ful. And
brought some corn for pop-ping. The

since we've no place to
lights are turned way down

go, let it snow, let it snow, let it snow. It
low; let it snow, let it snow, let it

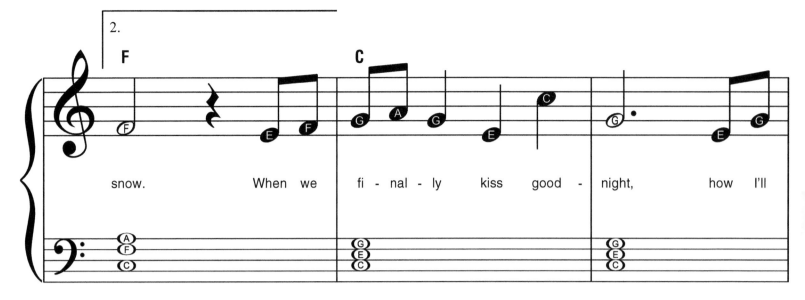

snow.   When we   fi - nal - ly   kiss   good - night,   how I'll

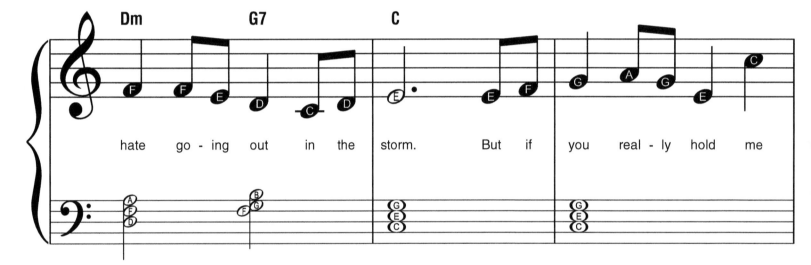

hate   go - ing   out   in   the   storm.   But   if   you   real - ly   hold   me

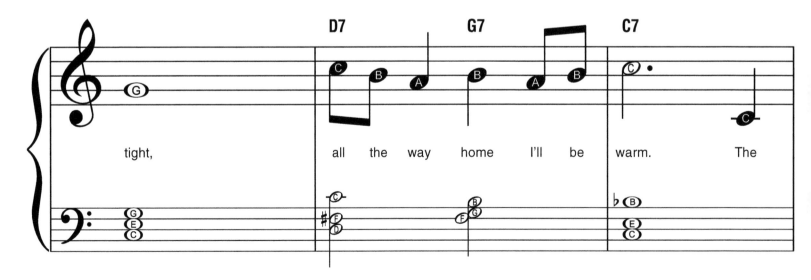

tight,   all   the   way   home   I'll   be   warm.   The

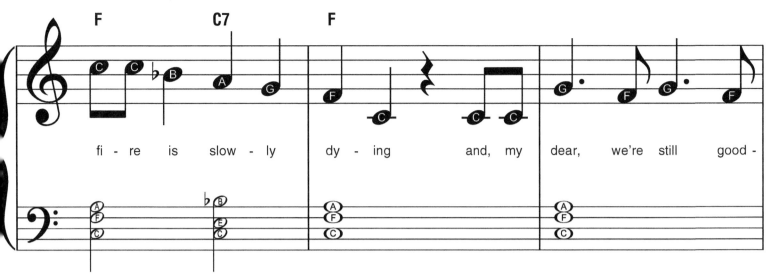

fi - re is slow - ly dy - ing and, my dear, we're still good-

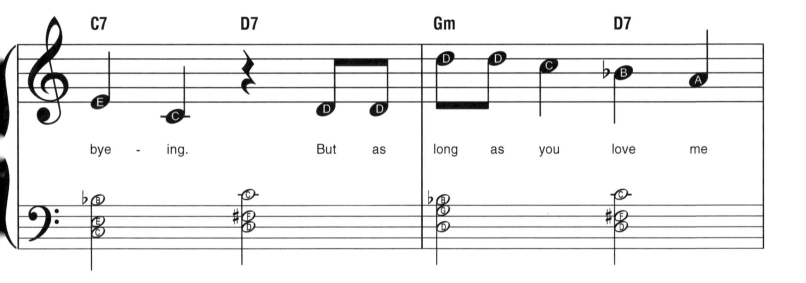

bye - ing. But as long as you love me

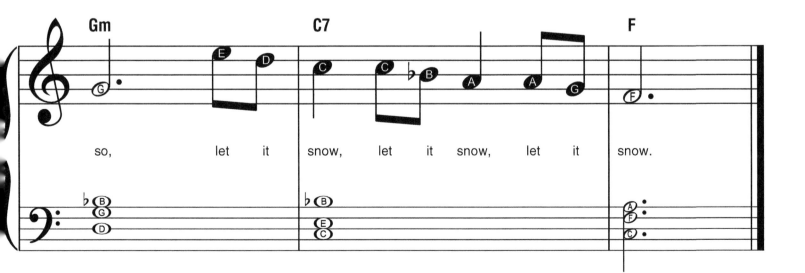

so, let it snow, let it snow, let it snow.

Mary, Did You Know?

Words and Music by Mark Lowry
and Buddy Greene

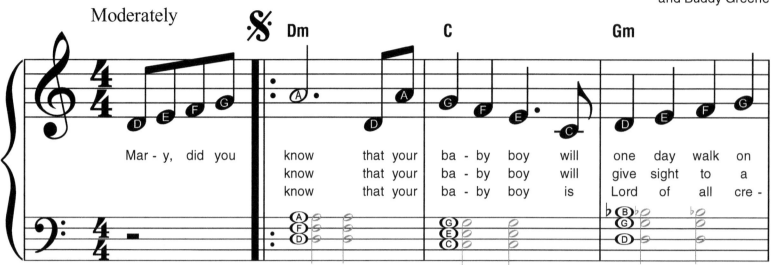

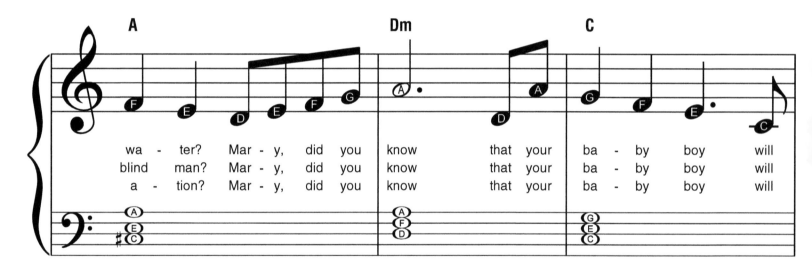

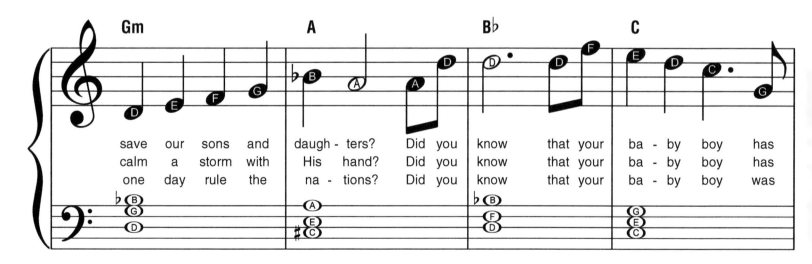

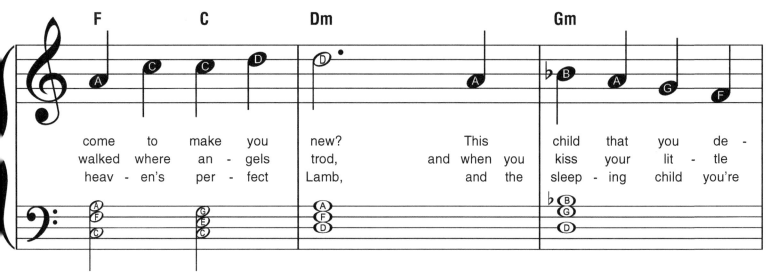

come to make you new? This child that you de -
walked where an - gels trod, and when you kiss your lit - tle
heav - en's per - fect Lamb, and the sleep - ing child you're

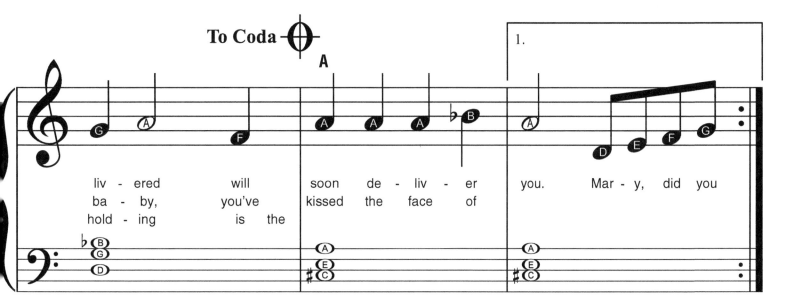

To Coda

1.

liv - ered will soon de - liv - er you. Mar - y, did you
ba - by, you've kissed the face of
hold - ing is the

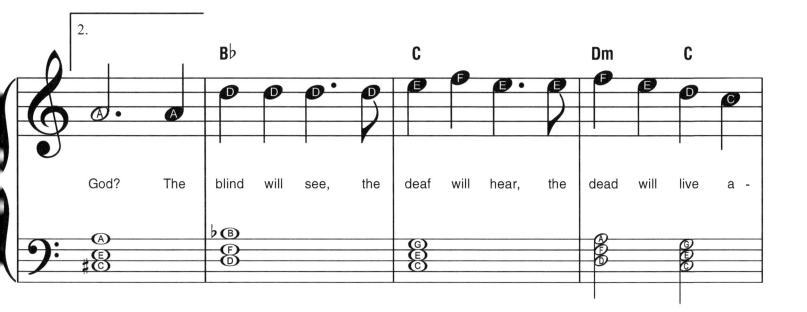

2.

God? The blind will see, the deaf will hear, the dead will live a -

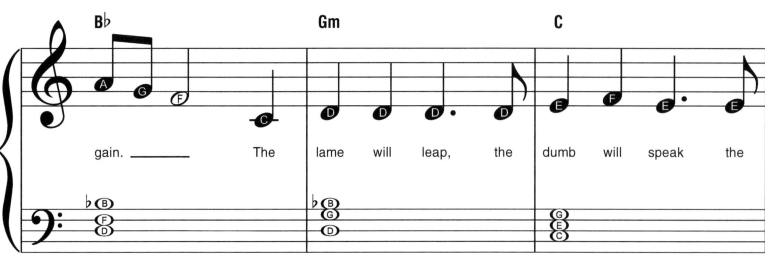

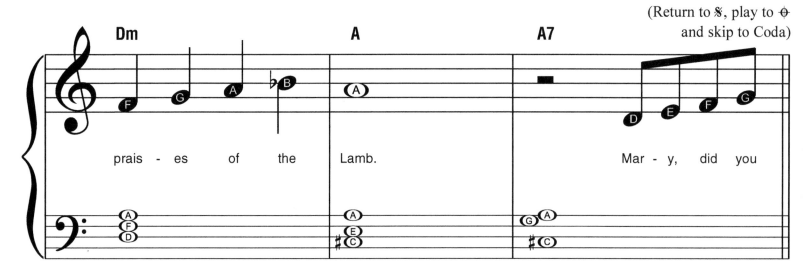

D.S. al Coda
(Return to 𝄋, play to 𝄌
and skip to Coda)

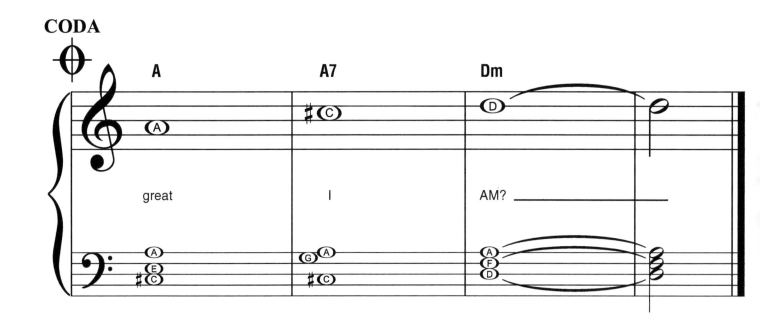

Merry Christmas, Darling

Words and Music by Richard Carpenter
and Frank Pooler

Moderately

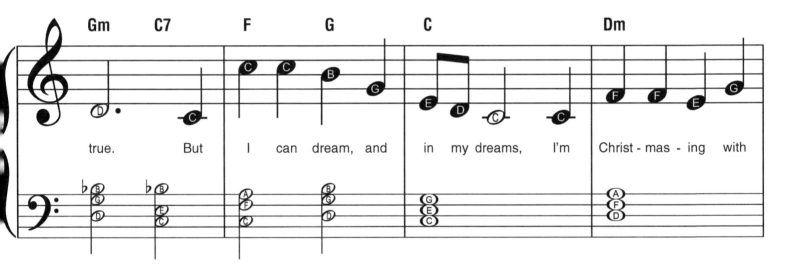

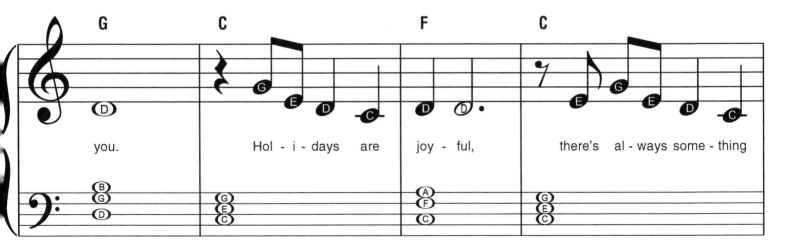

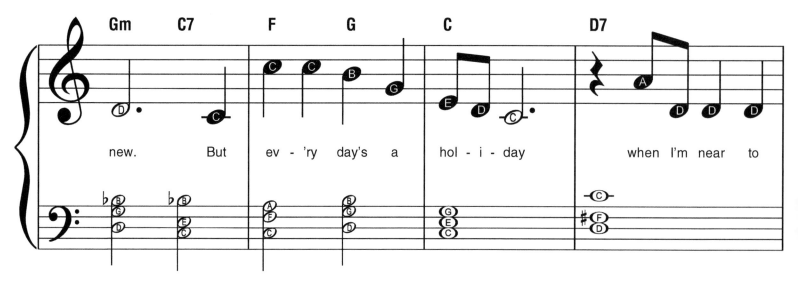

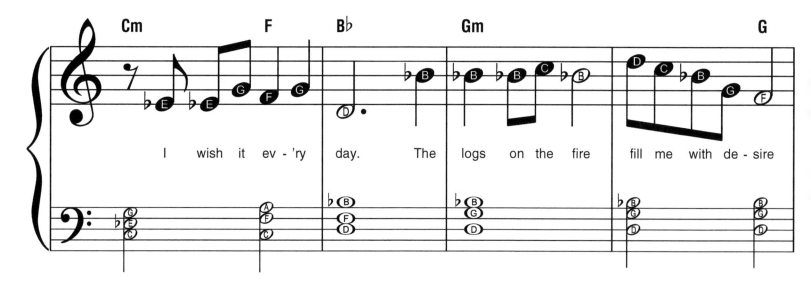

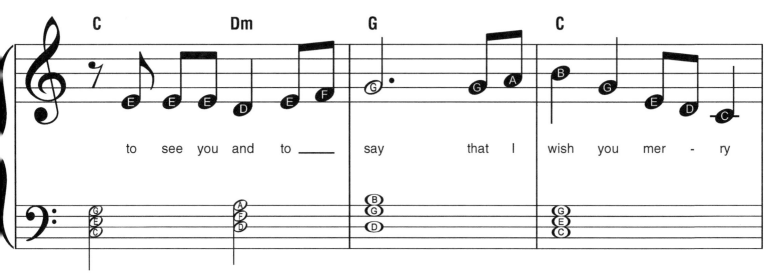

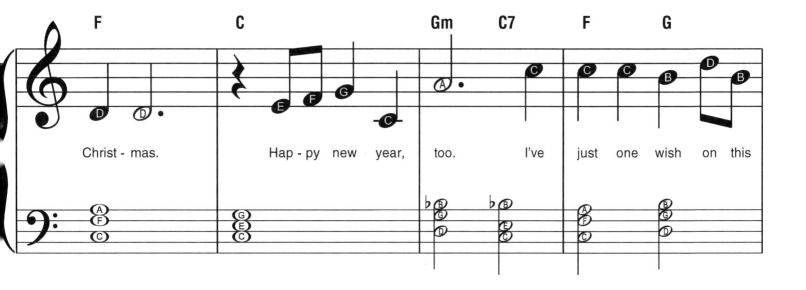

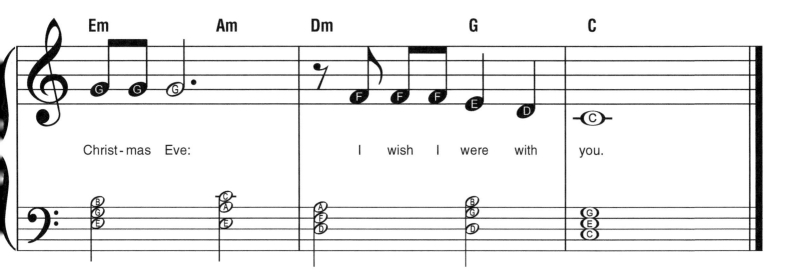

The Most Wonderful Time of the Year

Moderately, in 2

Words and Music by Eddie Pola
and George Wyle

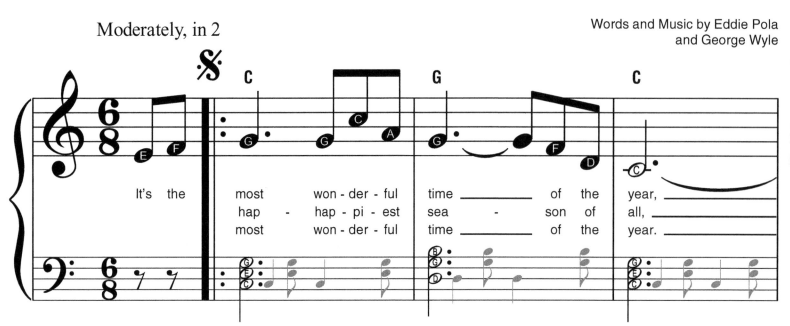

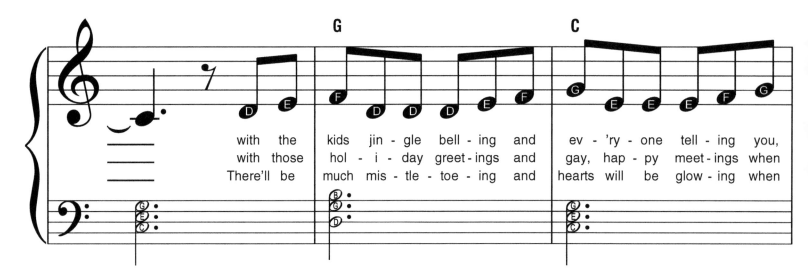

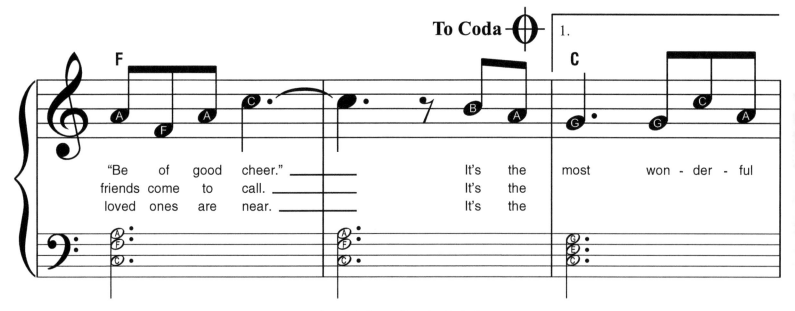

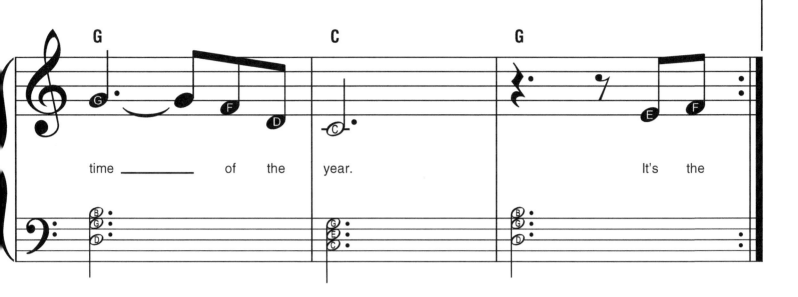

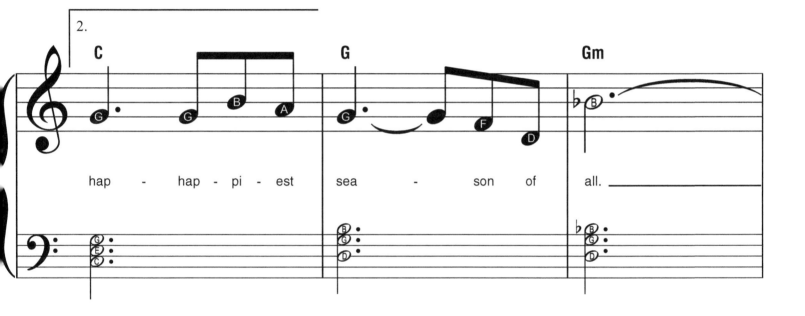

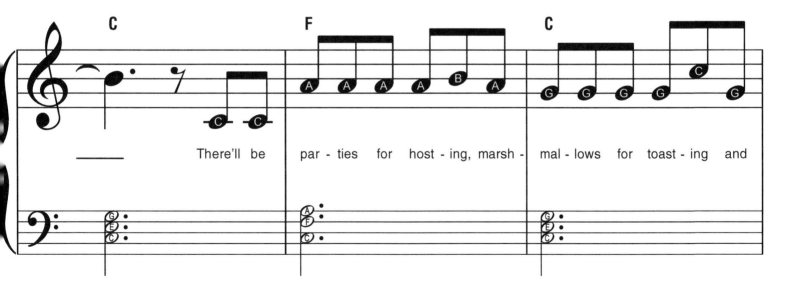

D.S. al Coda
(Return to 𝄋, play to ⊕
and skip to Coda)

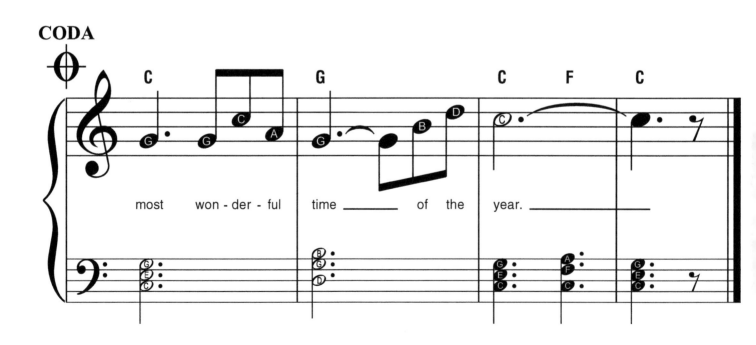

Rockin' Around the Christmas Tree

Music and Lyrics by
Johnny Marks

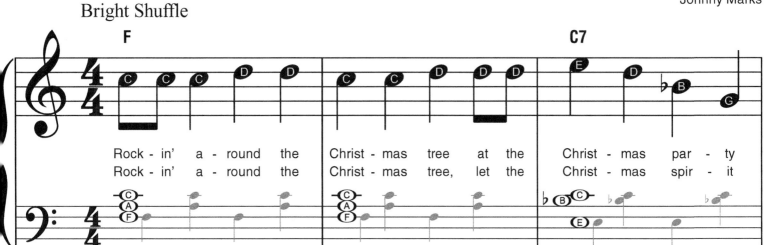

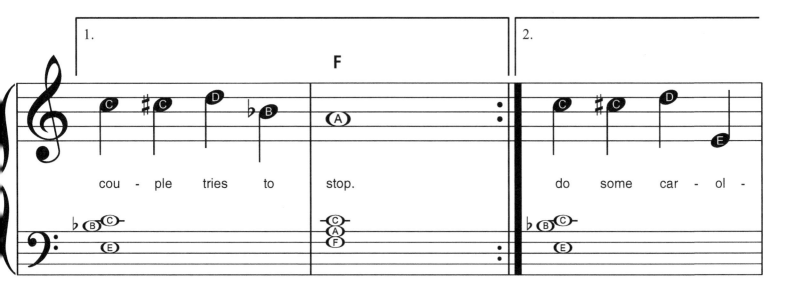

72

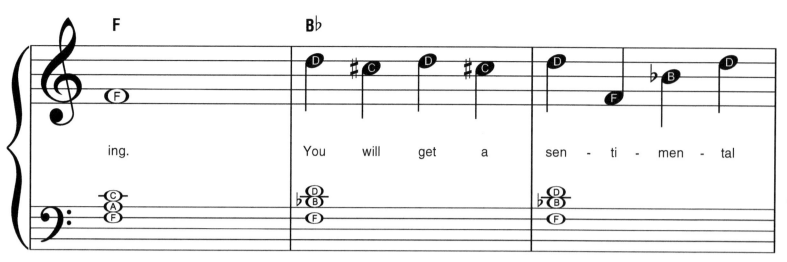

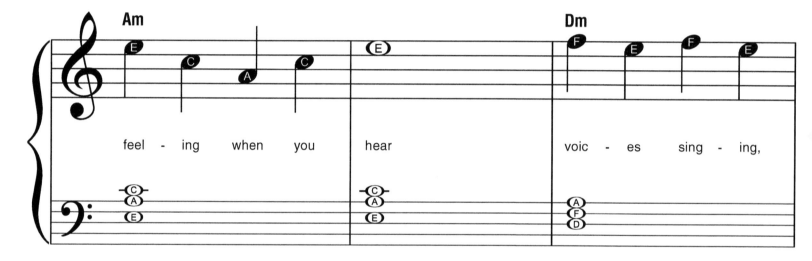

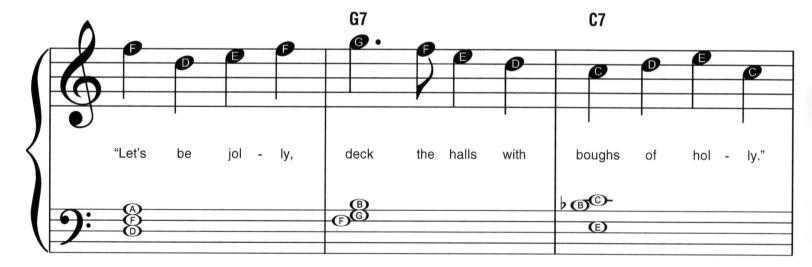

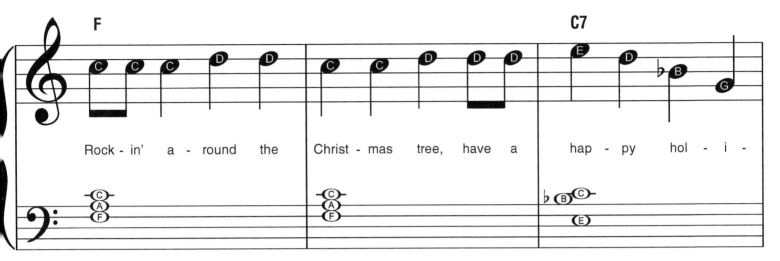

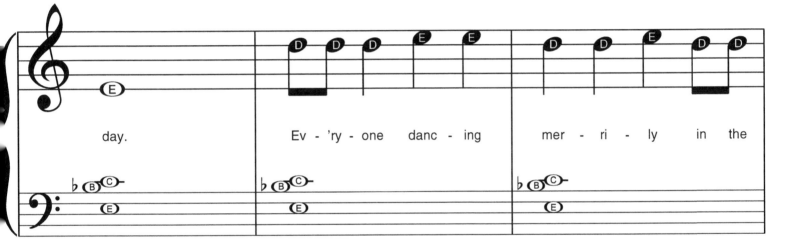

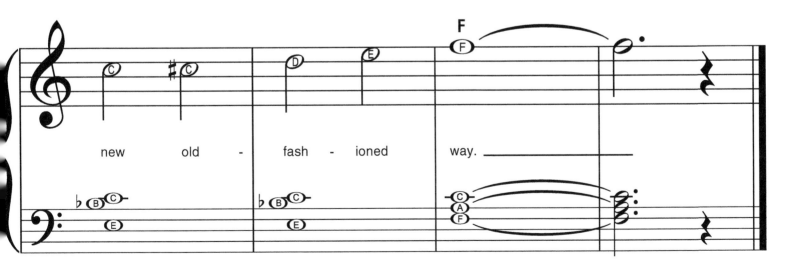

Rudolph the Red-Nosed Reindeer

Music and Lyrics by
Johnny Marks

Bright Shuffle

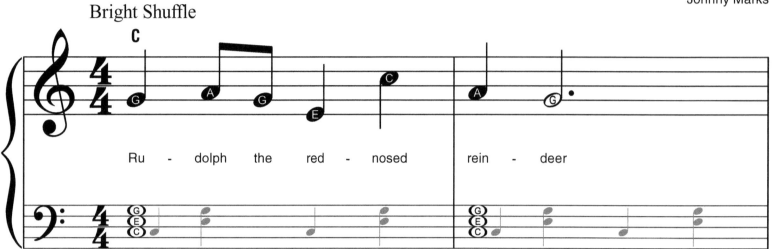

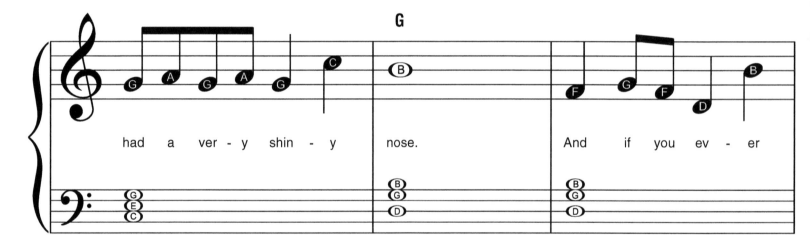

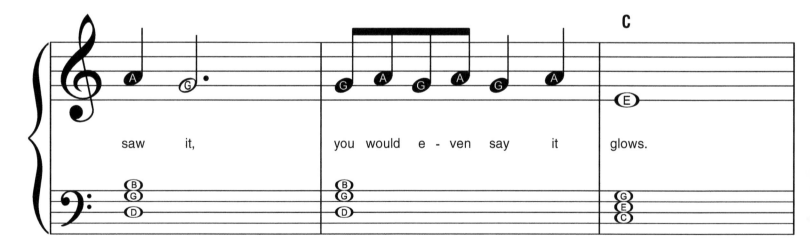

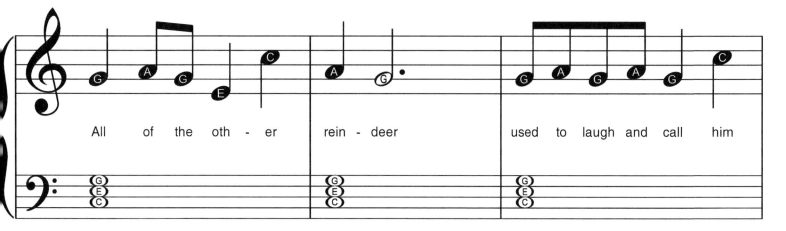

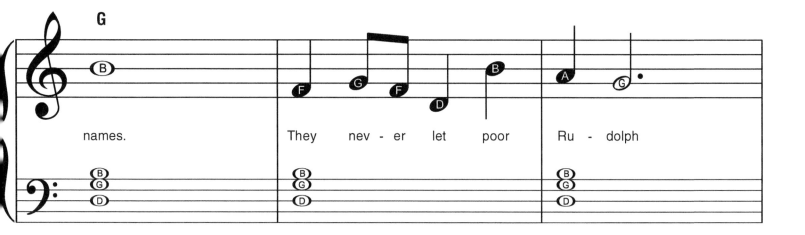

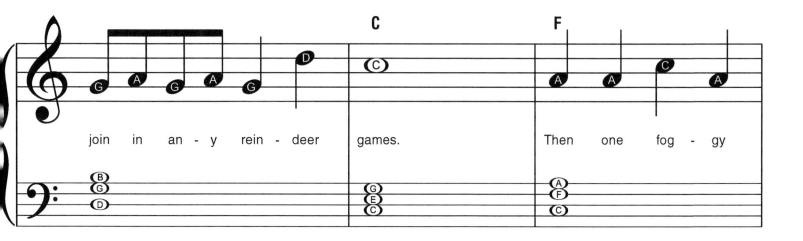

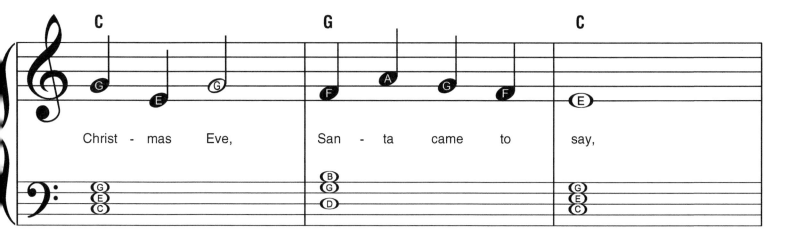

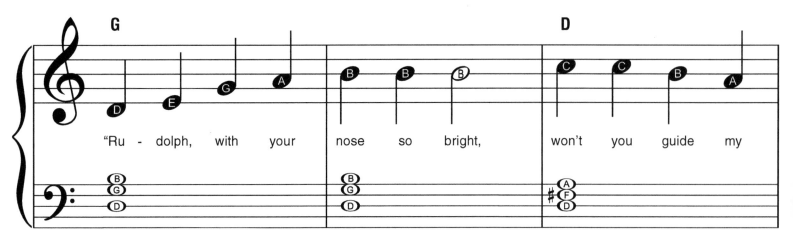

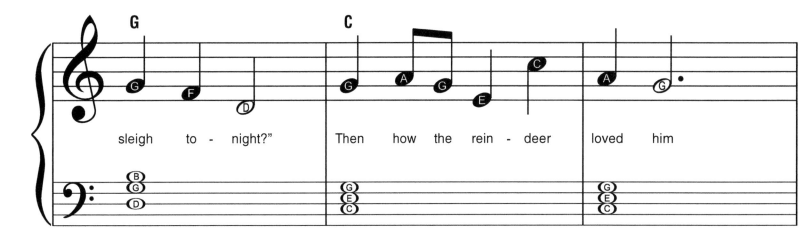

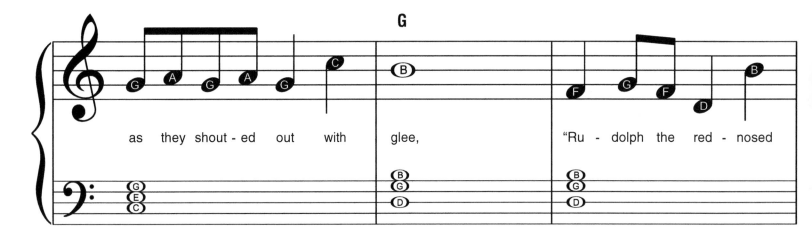

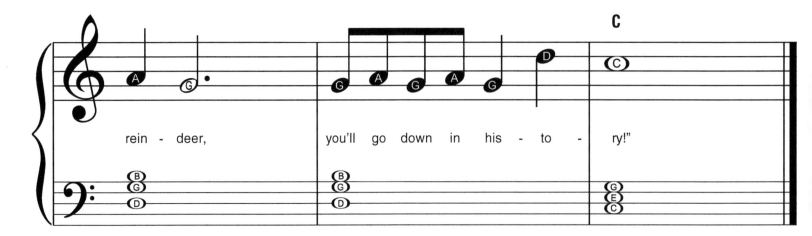

Santa Claus Is Comin' to Town

Words by Haven Gillespie
Music by J. Fred Coots

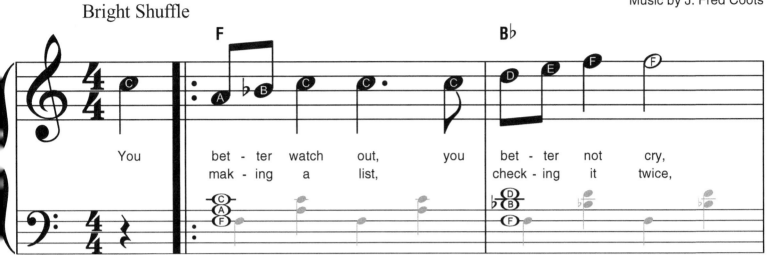

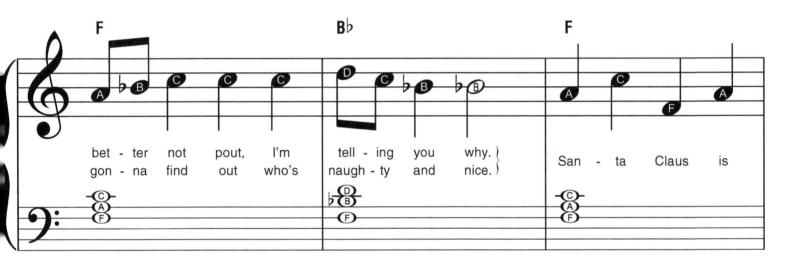

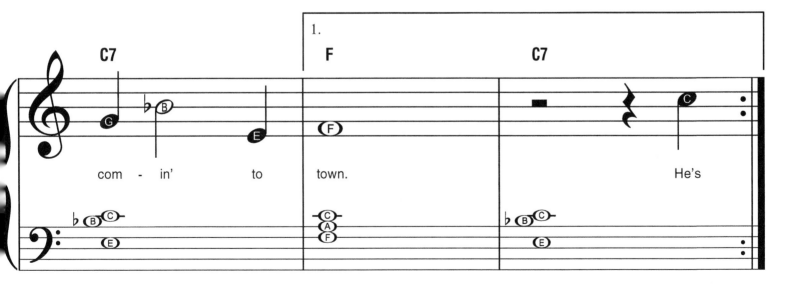

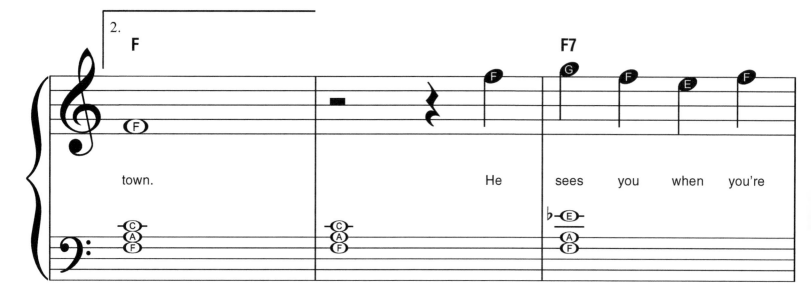

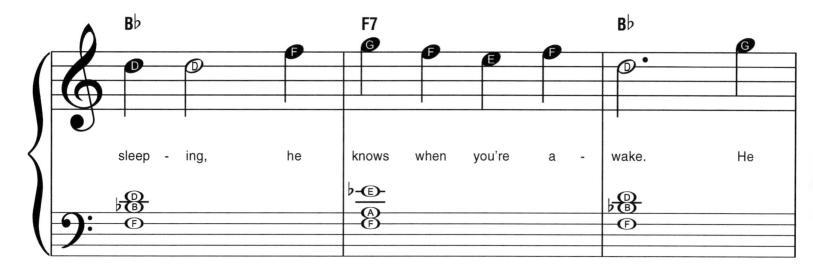

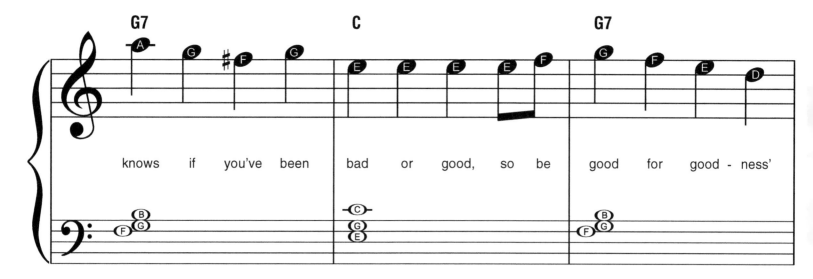

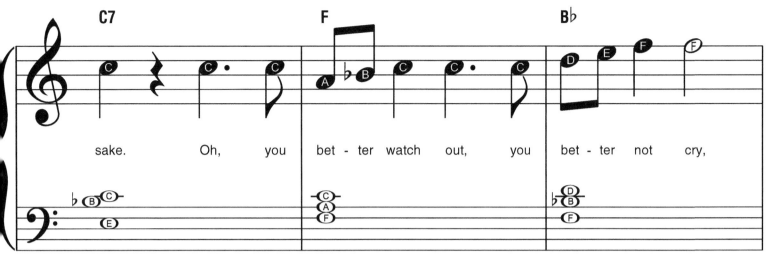

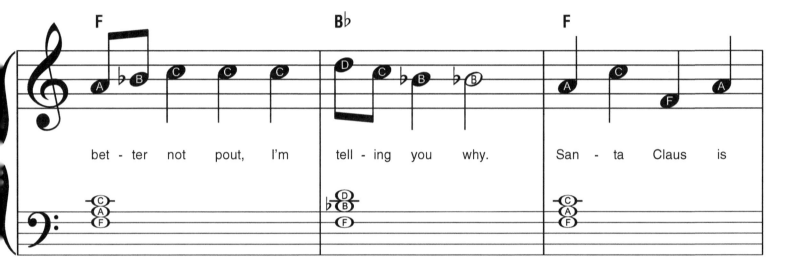

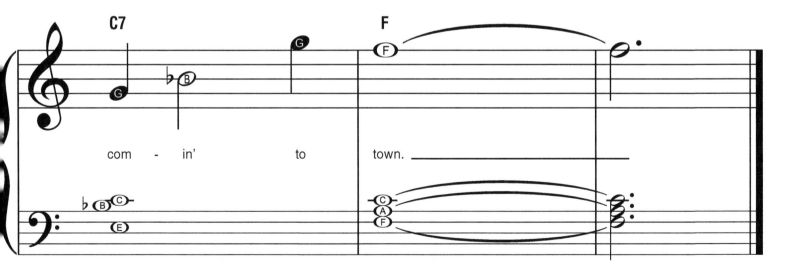

Silver Bells
from the Paramount Picture THE LEMON DROP KID

Words and Music by Jay Livingston
and Ray Evans

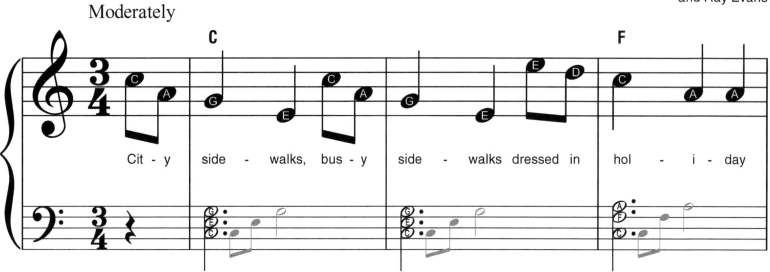

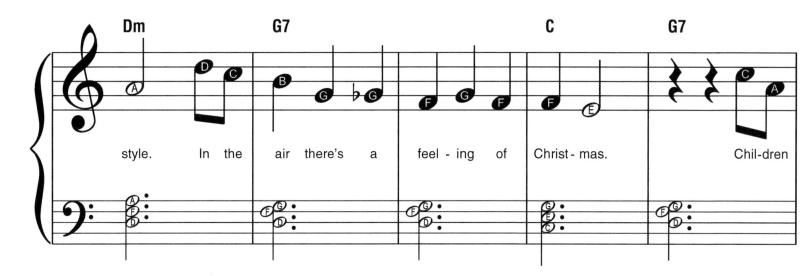

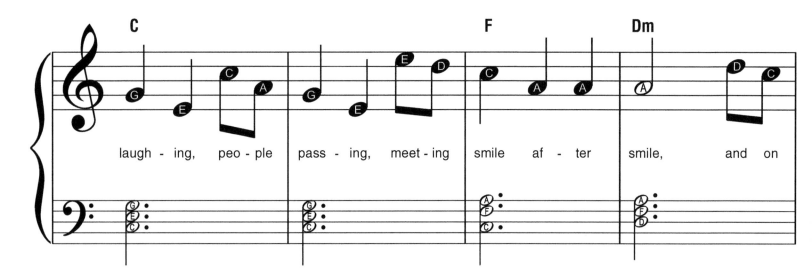

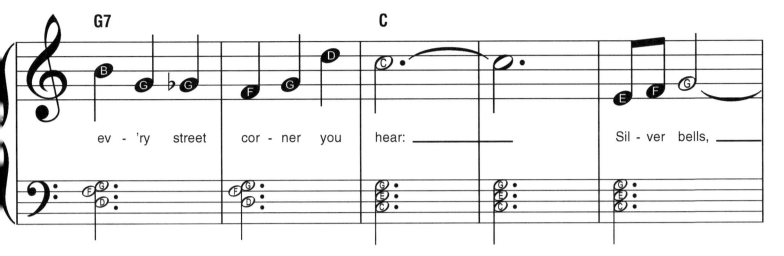

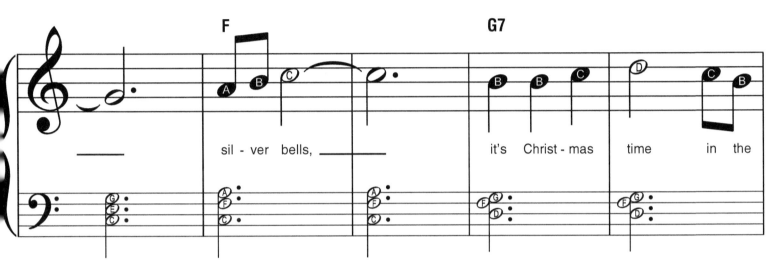

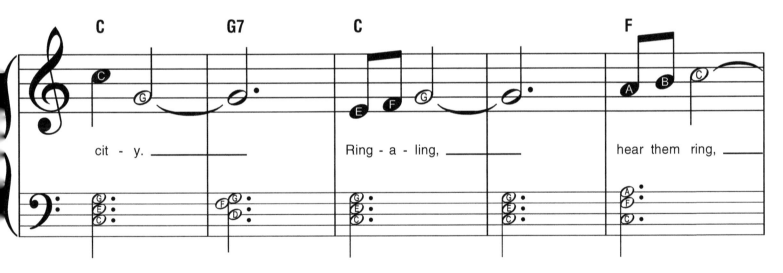

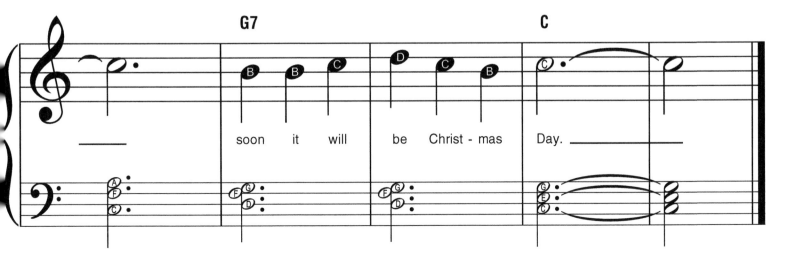

White Christmas
from the Motion Picture Irving Berlin's HOLIDAY INN

Words and Music by
Irving Berlin

Moderately

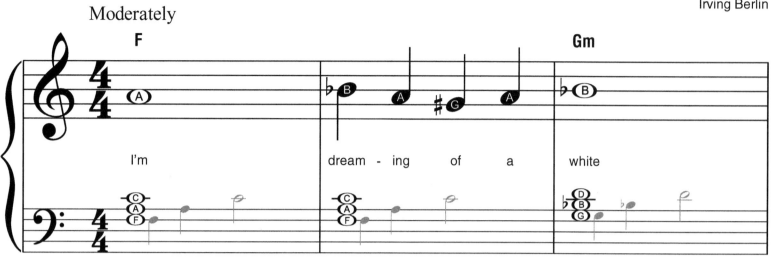

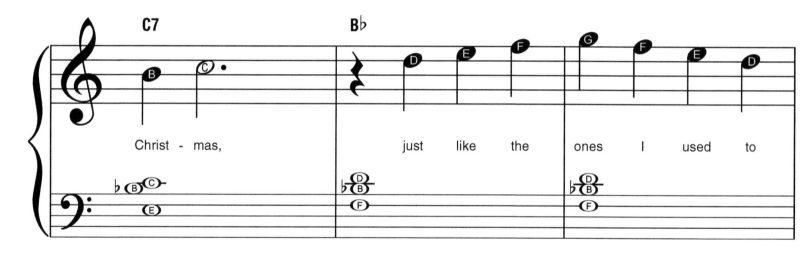

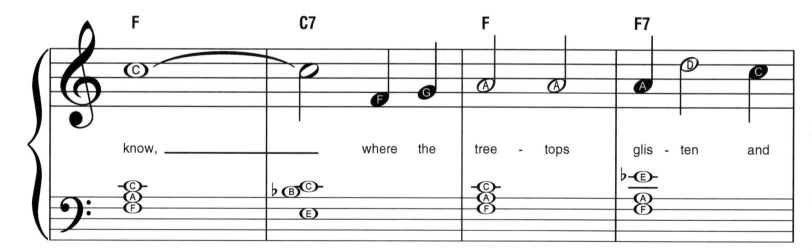

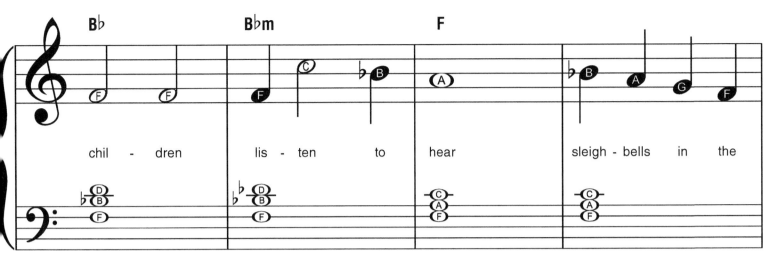

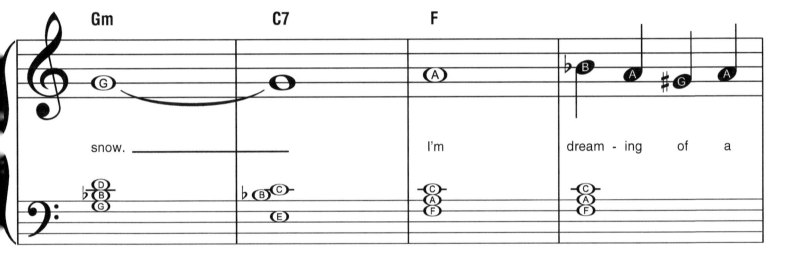

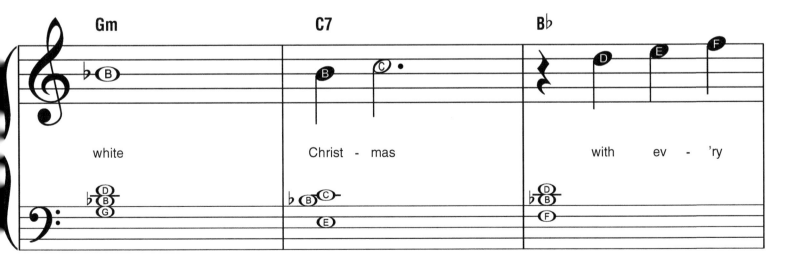

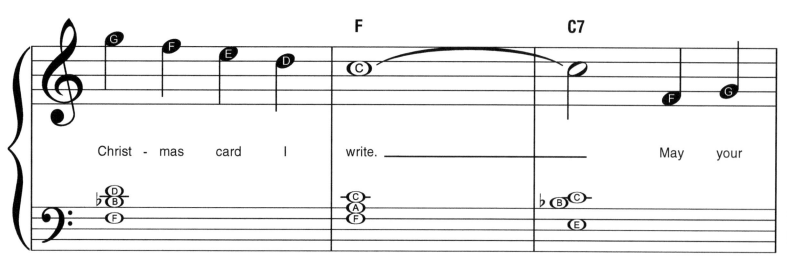

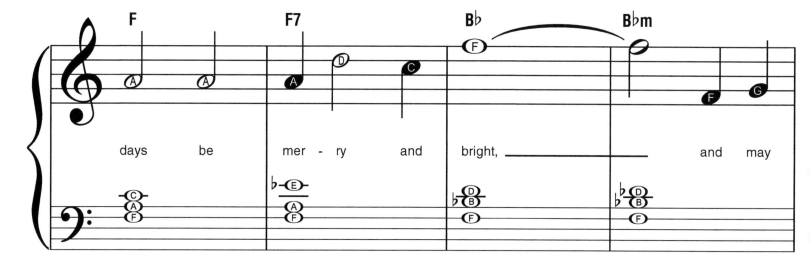

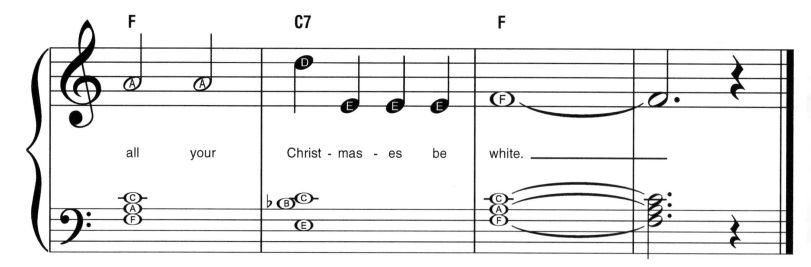

Winter Wonderland

Words by Dick Smith
Music by Felix Bernard

Moderate Shuffle

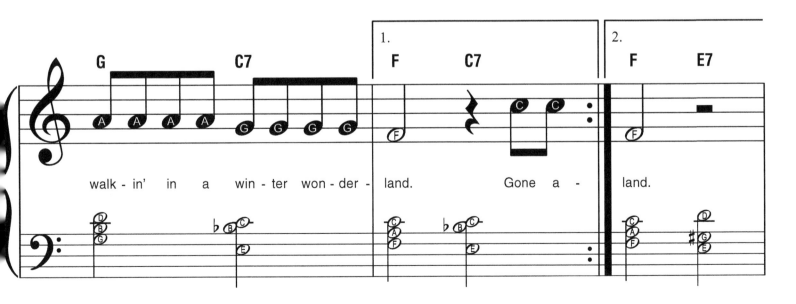

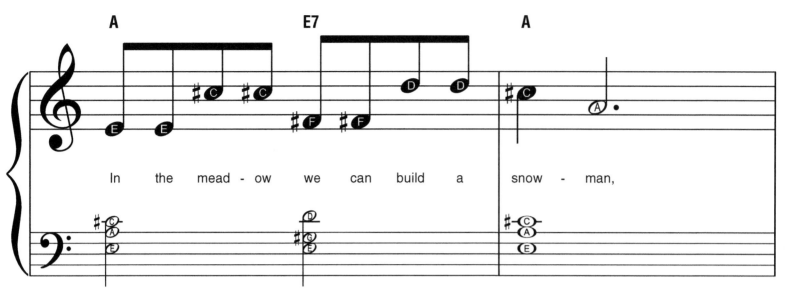

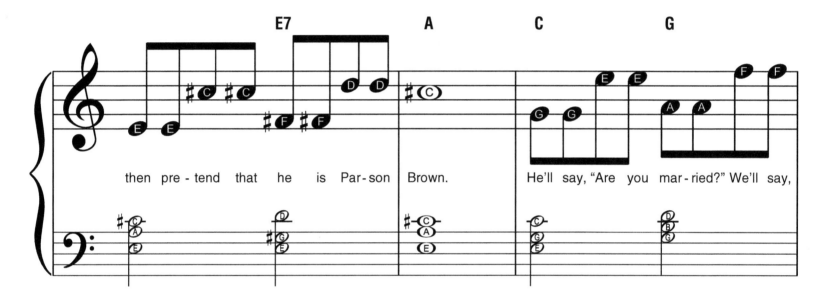

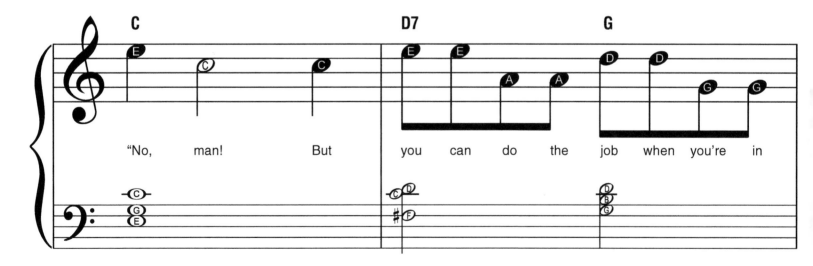

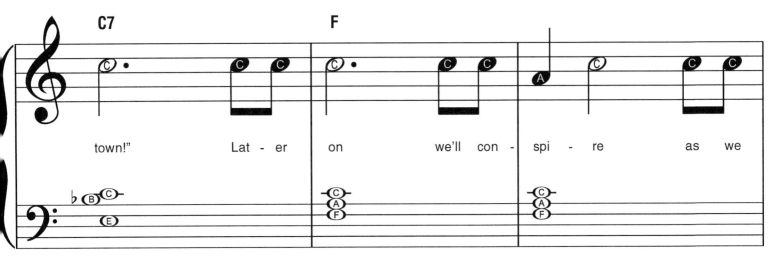

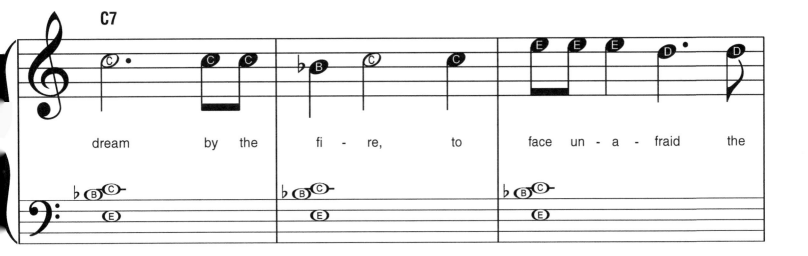

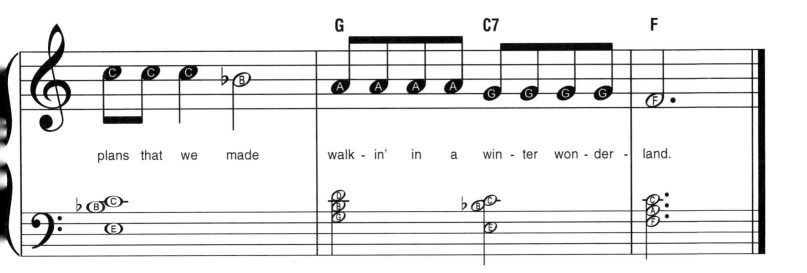

 **INSTANT Piano Songs**

The **Instant Piano Songs** series will help you play your favorite songs quickly and easily — whether you use one hand or two! Start with the melody in your right hand, adding basic left-hand chords when you're ready. Letter names inside each note speed up the learning process, and optional rhythm patterns take your playing to the next level. Online backing tracks are also included. Stream or download the tracks using the unique code inside each book, then play along to build confidence and sound great!

THE BEATLES

All My Loving • Blackbird • Can't Buy Me Love • Eleanor Rigby • Get Back • Here, There and Everywhere • Hey Jude • I Will • Let It Be • Michelle • Nowhere Man • Ob-La-Di, Ob-La-Da • Penny Lane • When I'm Sixty-Four • With a Little Help from My Friends • Yesterday • and more.
00295926 Book/Online Audio $14.99

BROADWAY'S BEST

All I Ask of You • Bring Him Home • Defying Gravity • Don't Cry for Me Argentina • Edelweiss • Memory • The Music of the Night • On My Own • People • Seasons of Love • Send in the Clowns • She Used to Be Mine • Sunrise, Sunset • Tonight • Waving Through a Window • and more.
00323342 Book/Online Audio $14.99

CHRISTMAS CLASSICS

Angels We Have Heard on High • Away in a Manger • Deck the Hall • The First Noel • Good King Wenceslas • Hark! the Herald Angels Sing • Jingle Bells • Jolly Old St. Nicholas • Joy to the World • O Christmas Tree • Up on the Housetop • We Three Kings of Orient Are • We Wish You a Merry Christmas • What Child Is This? • and more.
00348326 Book/Online Audio $14.99

CHRISTMAS STANDARDS

All I Want for Christmas Is You • Christmas Time Is Here • Frosty the Snow Man • Grown-Up Christmas List • A Holly Jolly Christmas • I'll Be Home for Christmas • Jingle Bell Rock • The Little Drummer Boy • Mary, Did You Know? • Merry Christmas, Darling • Rudolph the Red-Nosed Reindeer • White Christmas • and more.
00294854 Book/Online Audio $14.99

CLASSICAL THEMES

Canon (Pachelbel) • Für Elise (Beethoven) • Jesu, Joy of Man's Desiring (Bach) • Jupiter (Holst) • Lullaby (Brahms) • Pomp and Circumstance (Elgar) • Spring (Vivaldi) • Symphony No. 9, Fourth Movement ("Ode to Joy") (Beethoven) • and more.
00283826 Book/Online Audio $14.99

DISNEY FAVORITES

Beauty and the Beast • Can You Feel the Love Tonight • Chim Chim Cher-ee • Colors of the Wind • A Dream Is a Wish Your Heart Makes • Friend Like Me • How Far I'll Go • It's a Small World • Kiss the Girl • Lava • Let It Go • Mickey Mouse March • Part of Your World • Reflection • Remember Me (Ernesto de la Cruz) • A Whole New World • You'll Be in My Heart (Pop Version) • and more.
00283720 Book/Online Audio $14.99

HITS OF 2010-2019 – INSTANT PIANO SONGS

All About That Bass (Meghan Trainor) • All of Me (John Legend) • Can't Stop the Feeling (Justin Timberlake) • Happy (Pharrell Williams) • Hey, Soul Sister (Train) • Just the Way You Are (Bruno Mars) • Rolling in the Deep (Adele) • Shallow (Lady Gaga & Bradley Cooper) • Shake It Off (Taylor Swift) • Shape of You (Ed Sheeran) • and more.
00345364 Book/Online Audio $14.99

MOVIE SONGS

As Time Goes By • City of Stars • Endless Love • Hallelujah • I Will Always Love You • Laura • Moon River • My Heart Will Go on (Love Theme from 'Titanic') • Over the Rainbow • Singin' in the Rain • Skyfall • Somewhere Out There • Stayin' Alive • Tears in Heaven • Unchained Melody • Up Where We Belong • The Way We Were • What a Wonderful World • and more.
00283718 Book/Online Audio $14.99

POP HITS

All of Me • Chasing Cars • Despacito • Feel It Still • Havana • Hey, Soul Sister • Ho Hey • I'm Yours • Just Give Me a Reason • Love Yourself • Million Reasons • Perfect • Riptide • Shake It Off • Stay with Me • Thinking Out Loud • Viva La Vida • What Makes You Beautiful • and more.
00283825 Book/Online Audio $14.99

SONGS FOR KIDS – INSTANT PIANO SONGS

Do-Re-Mi • Hakuna Matata • It's a Small World • On Top of Spaghetti • Puff the Magic Dragon • The Rainbow Connection • SpongeBob SquarePants Theme Song • Take Me Out to the Ball Game • Tomorrow • The Wheels on the Bus • Won't You Be My Neighbor? (It's a Beautiful Day in the Neighborhood) • You Are My Sunshine • and more.
00323352 Book/Online Audio $14.99

 **HAL•LEONARD®**
www.halleonard.com